D0189682

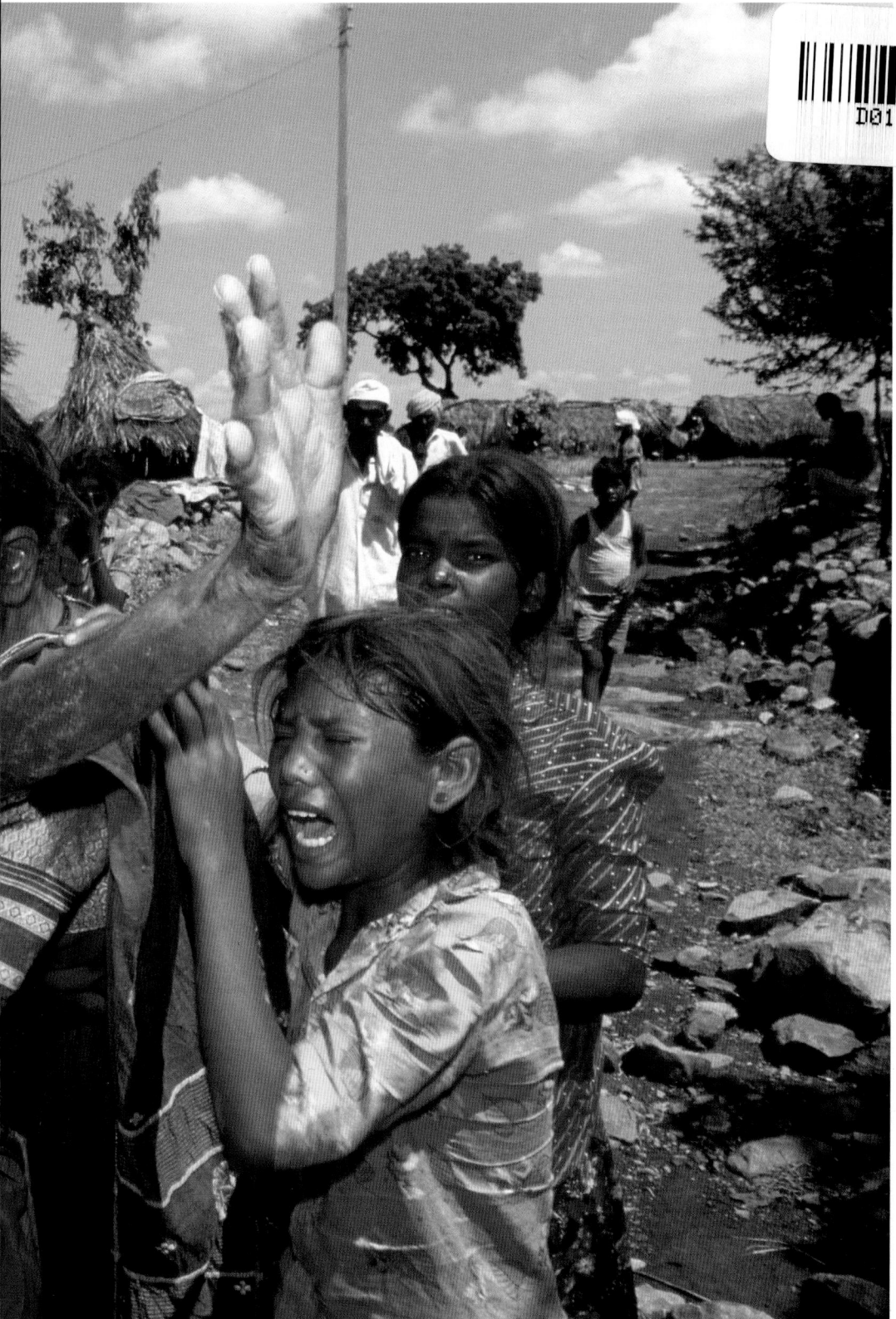

SWAPAN PAREKH
India,
Black Star,
USA

**FIRST PRIZE
SINGLES**

9402

9402
Although the earthquake that hit Latur in the central Indian state of Maharashtra on September 30 registered 'only' 6.4 on the Richter scale, it flattened a large, densely populated area. Claiming some 15,000 lives and leaving 65,000 homeless, it was the worst such disaster to hit the subcontinent in decades.

Above, a woman who has lost her three children shares her grief with other survivors. Hers was one of many families who perished, buried as they lay sleeping in their mud brick houses. Having initially declined offers of help from abroad, India later accepted foreign relief supplies for the first time since its independence in 1947.

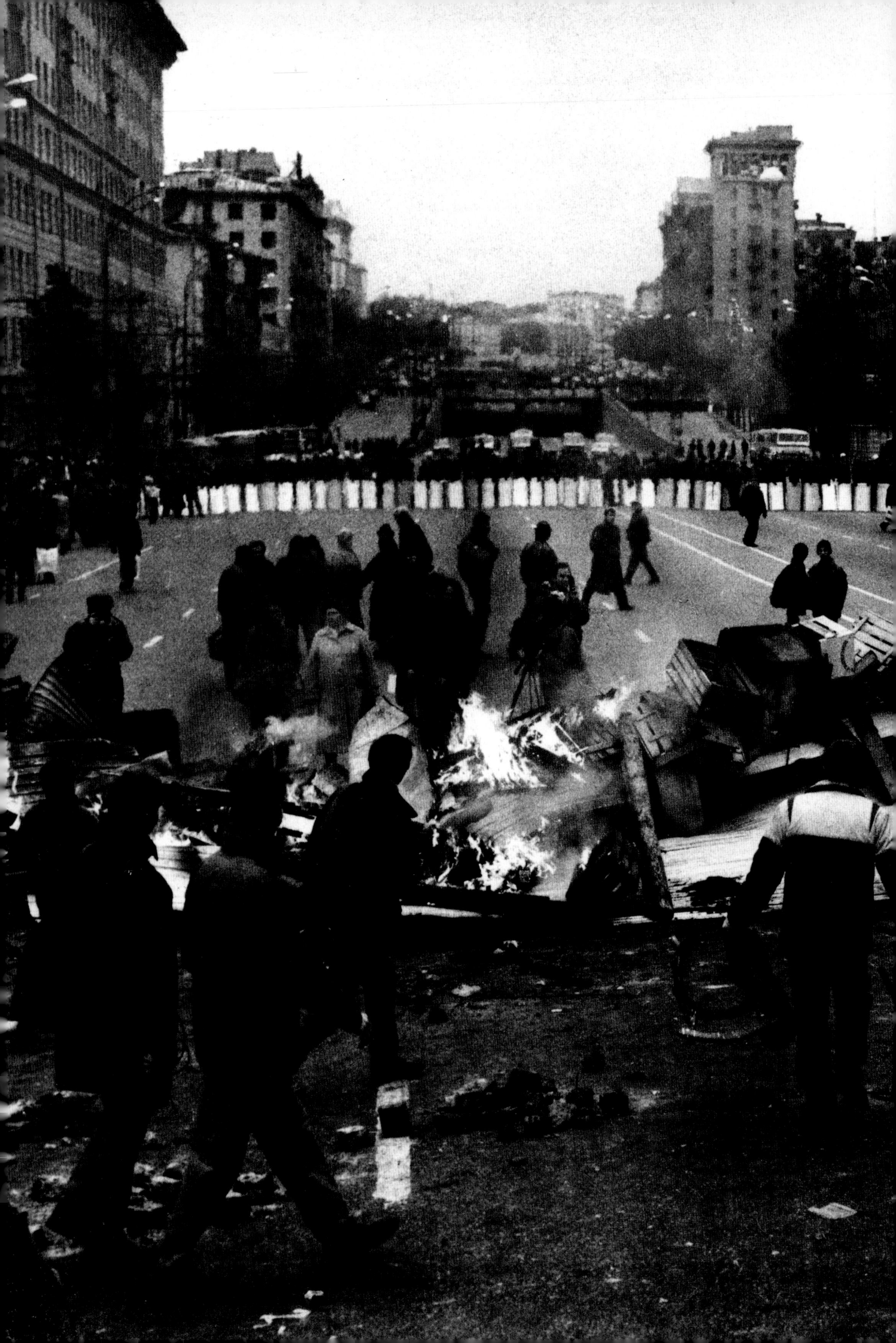

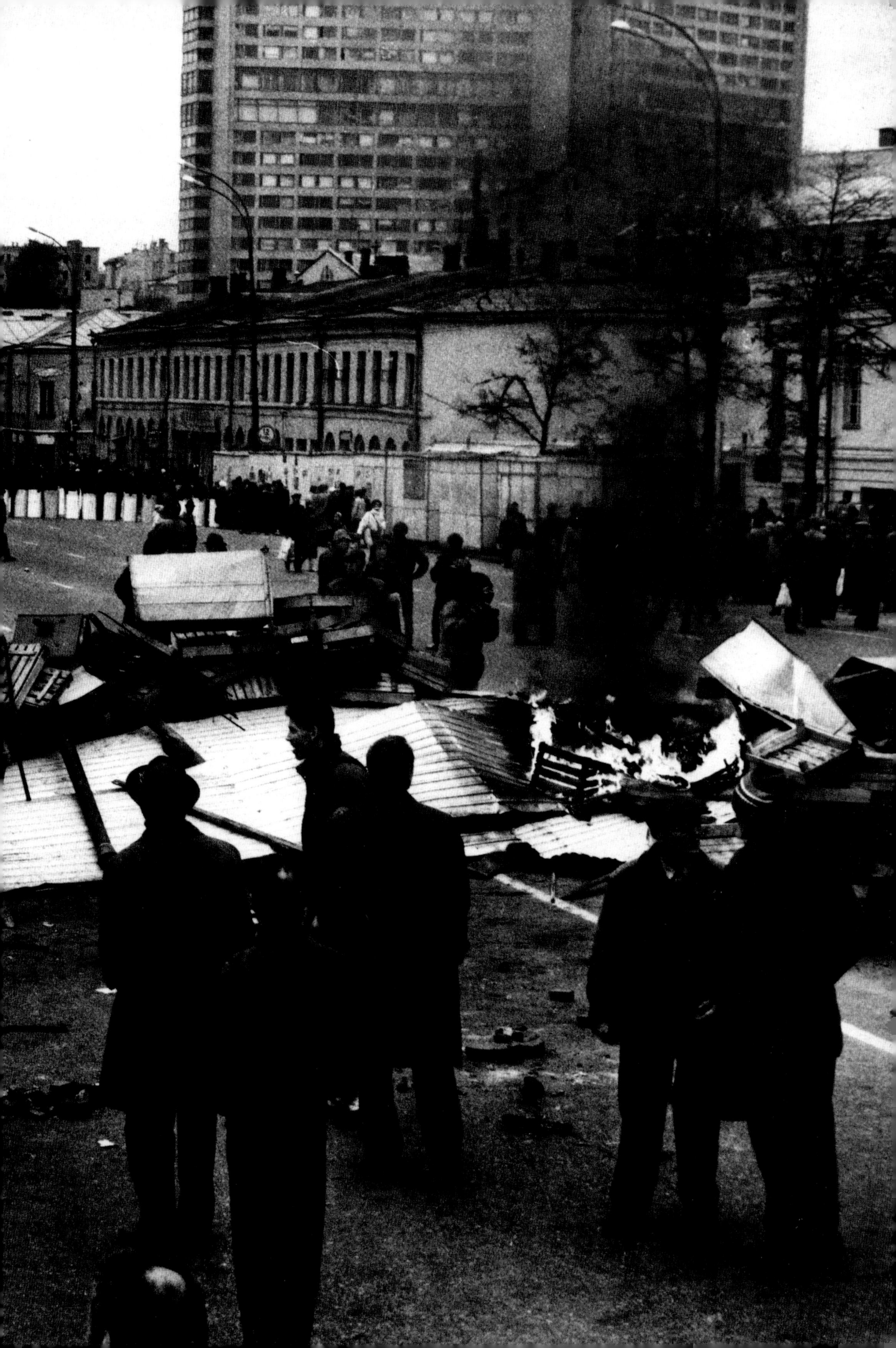

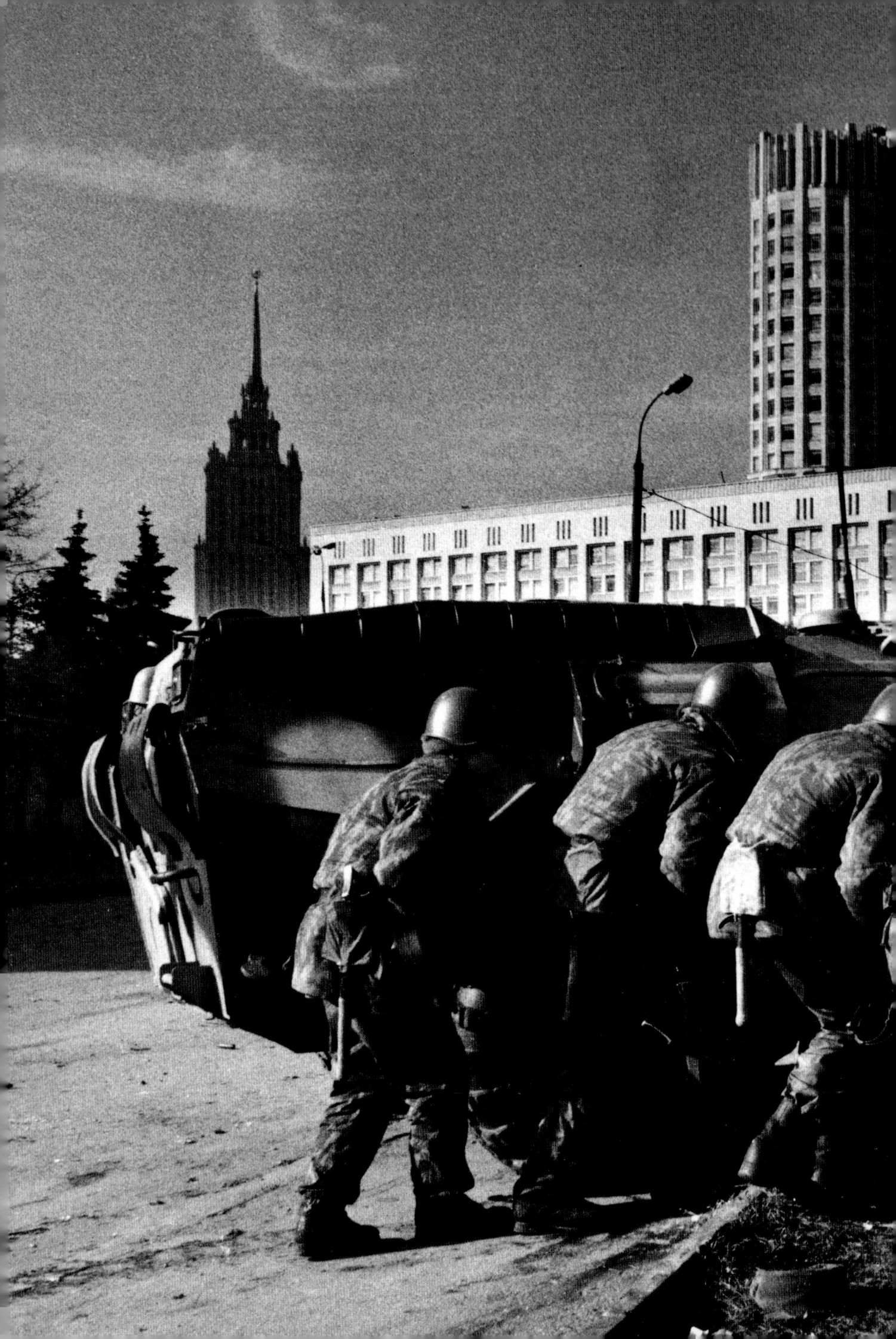

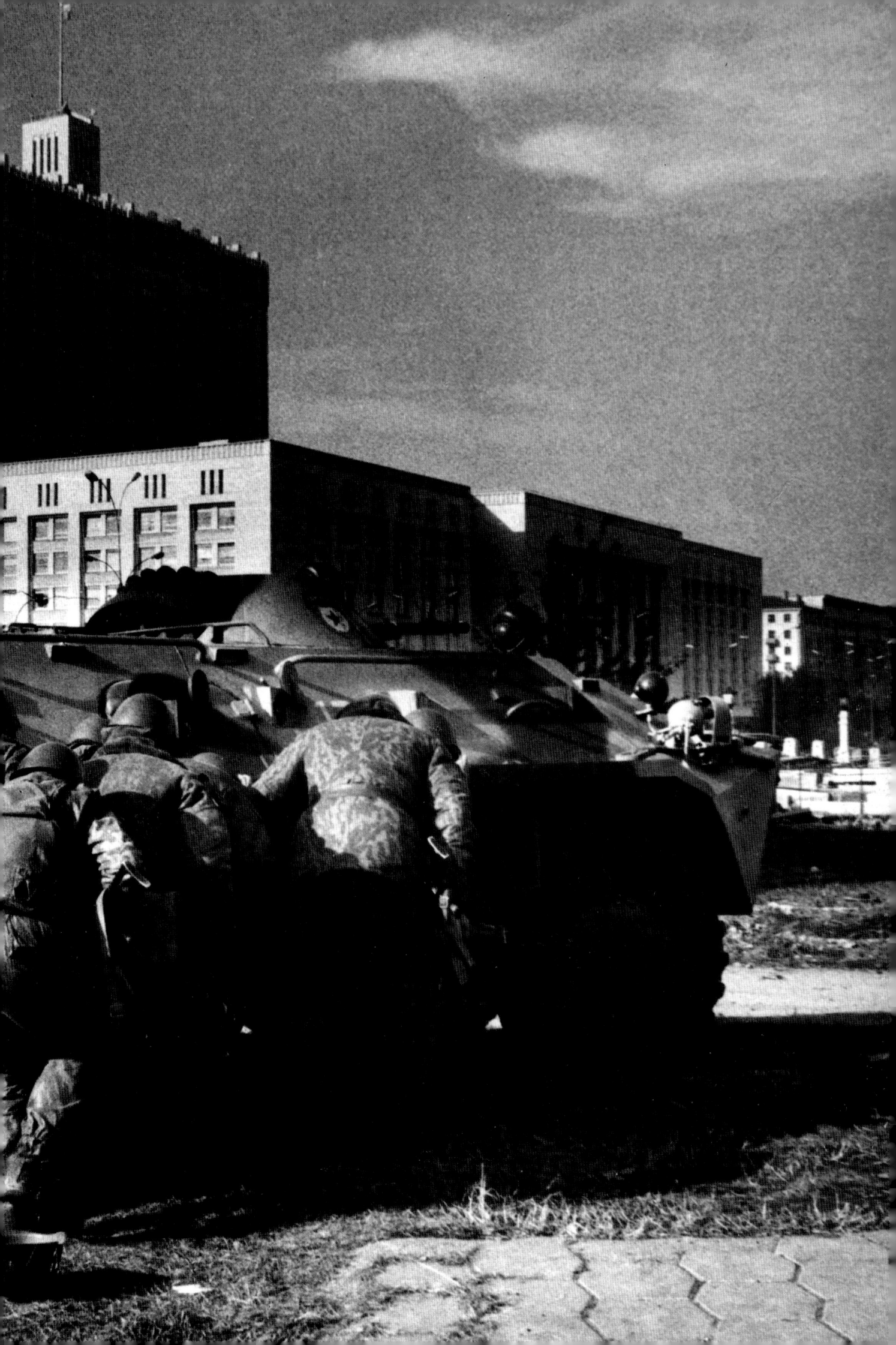

EDWARD OPP
USA,
Primus
Photo Agency,
Russia

**SECOND PRIZE
STORIES**

9403

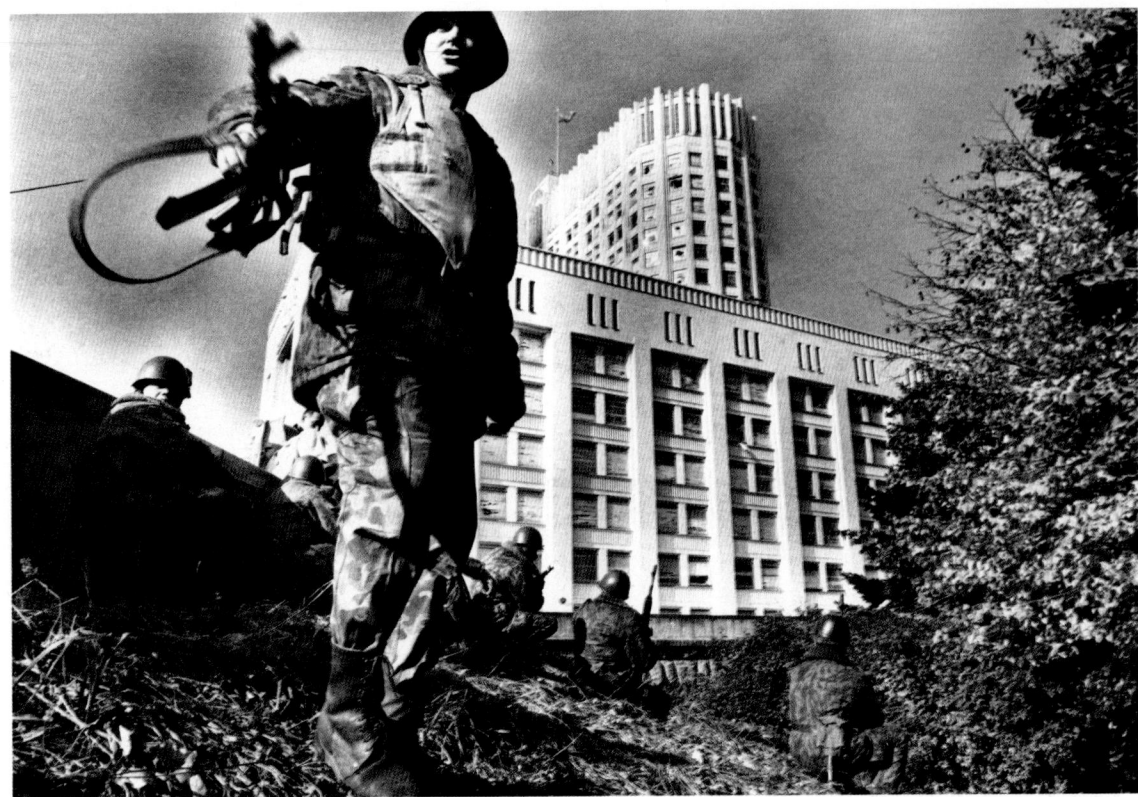

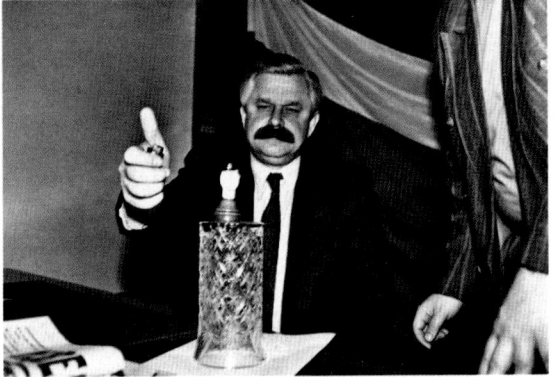

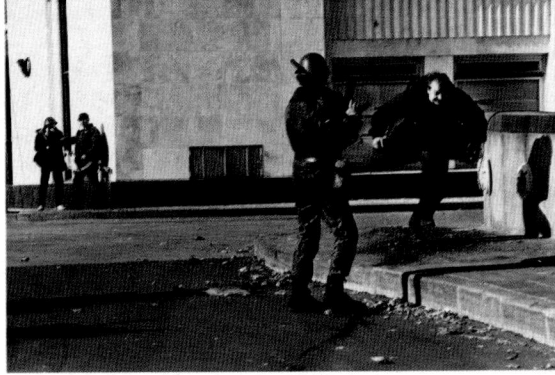

9403 (story starts on p.12)
The power struggle between Russia's legislature, led by Ruslan Khasbulatov and Aleksandr Rutskoi, and President Yeltsin came to a head when Yeltsin dissolved parliament on September 21. As the world looked on, the rebels barricaded themselves in Moscow's White House parliament building, where they installed Rutskoi (above) as their new president.

Page 12: Barricades are erected on Moscow's main street. When soldiers and tanks appeared on the scene, they became targets for sniper fire from the White House (page 14). In the afternoon of October 4 the rebels, some of them injured (far right), started evacuating the building. Storm troops reclaiming the White House for Yeltsin found more than 40 bodies.

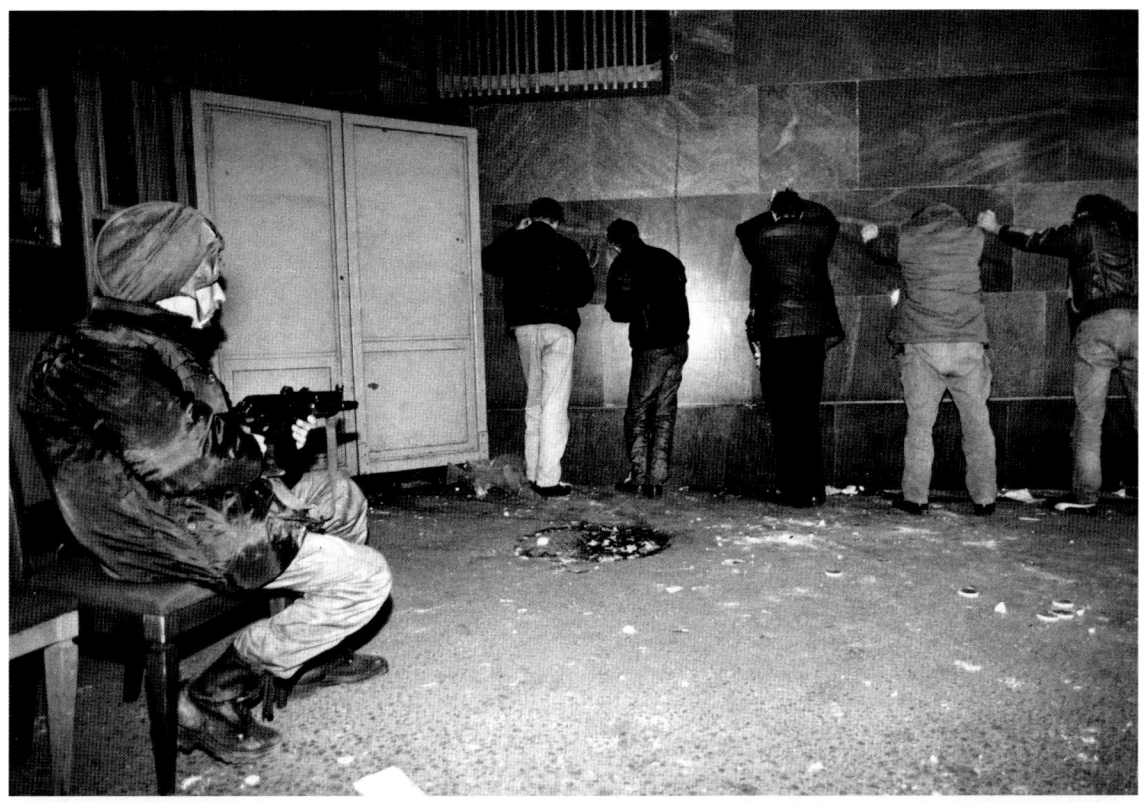

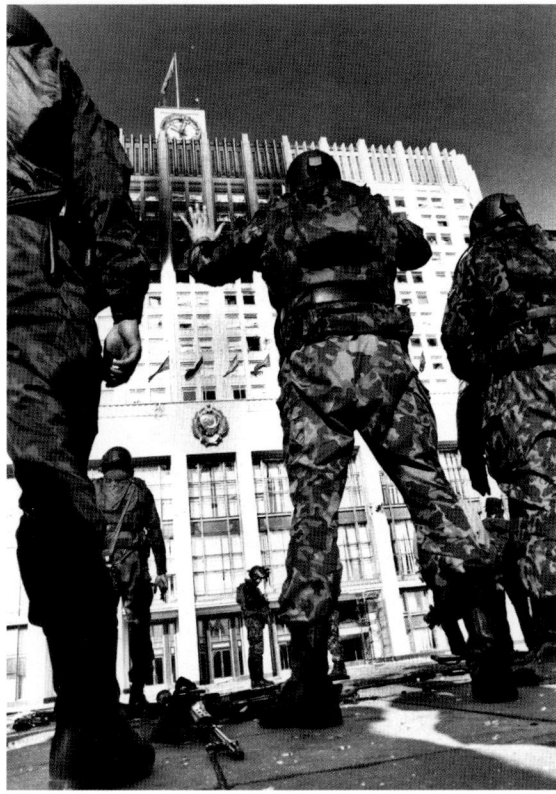

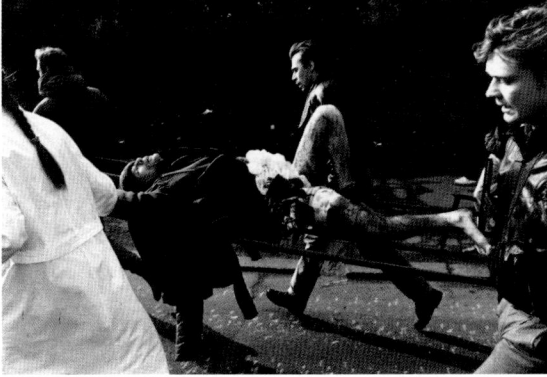

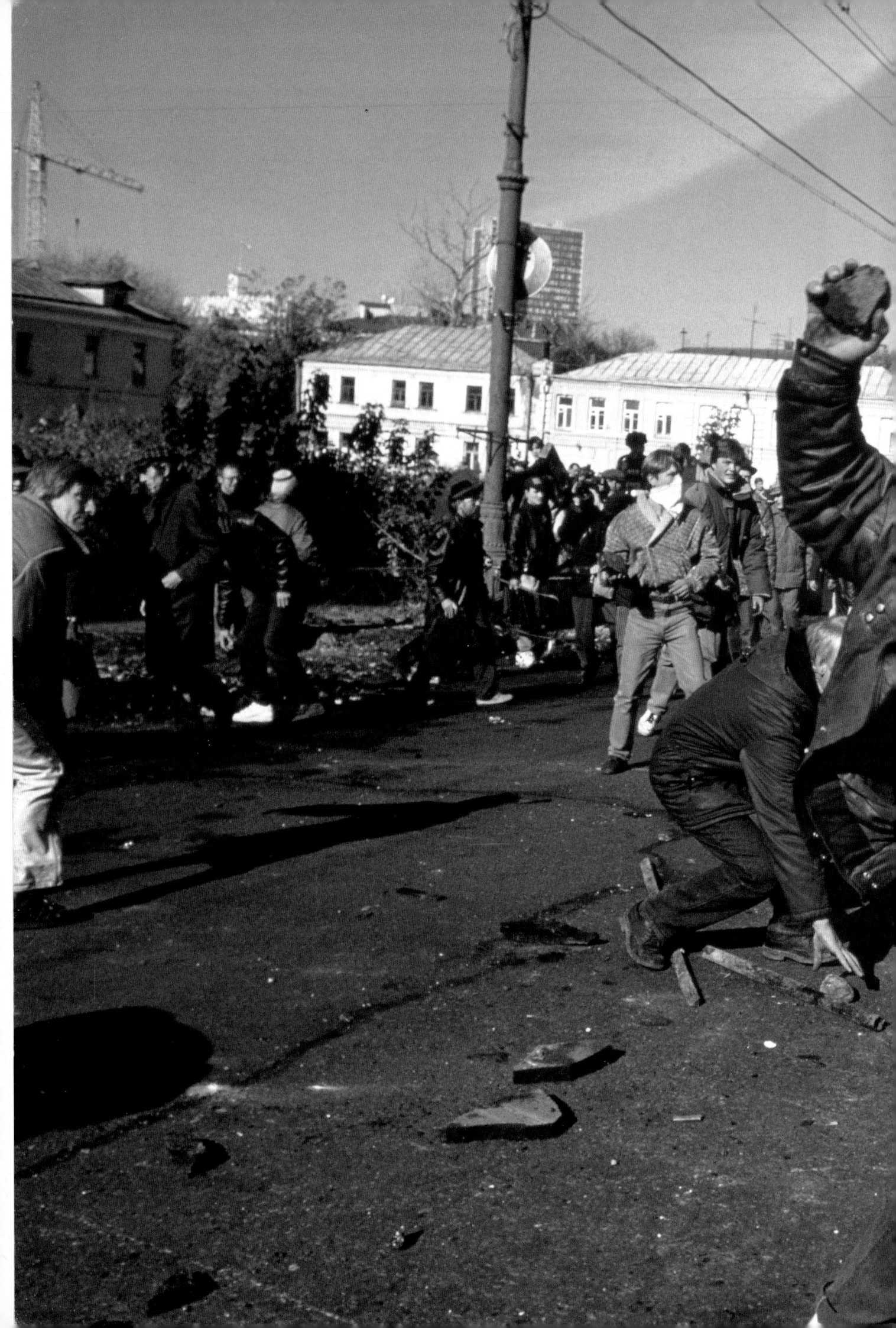

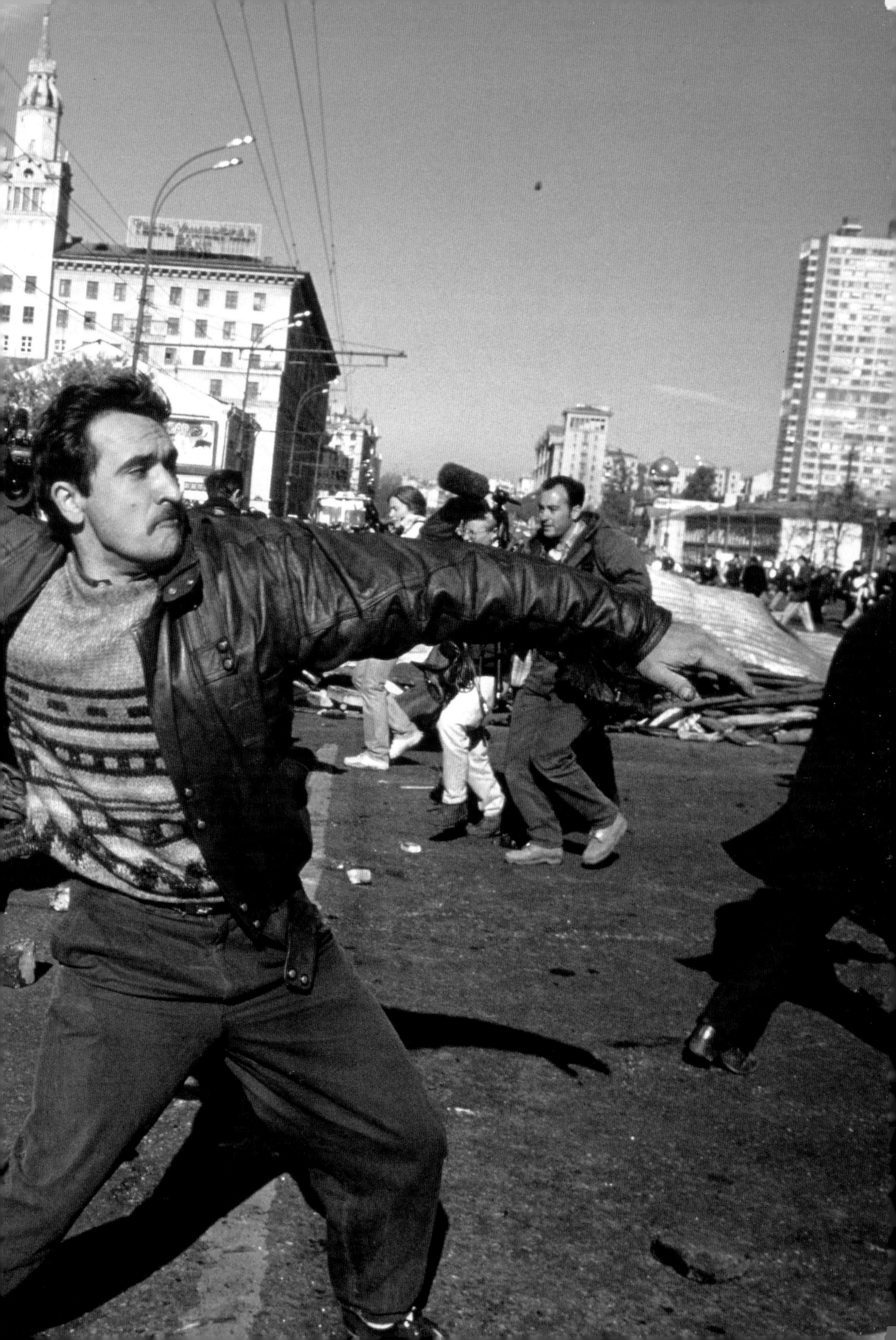

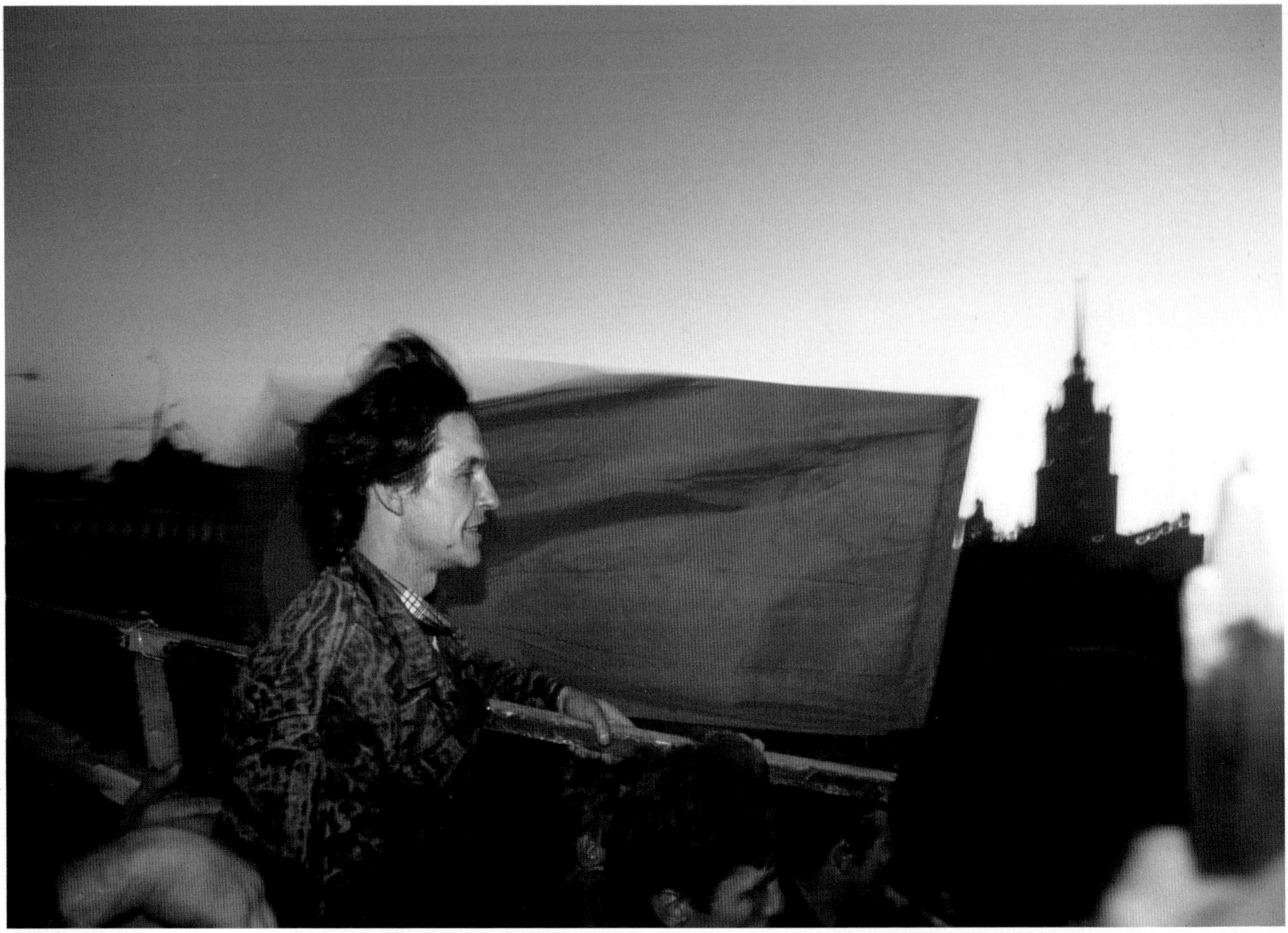

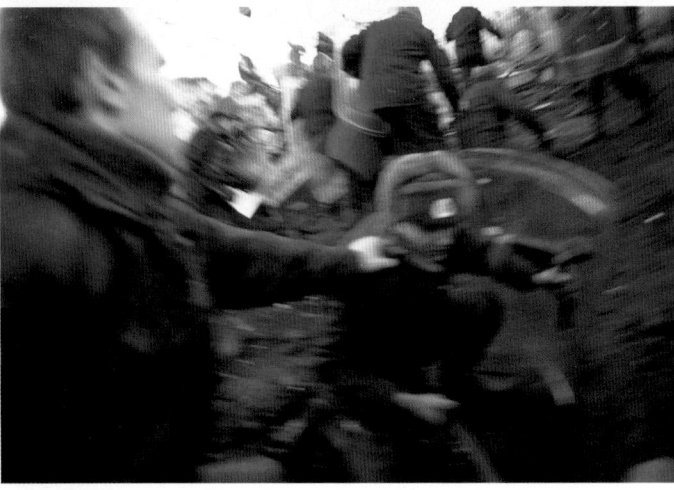

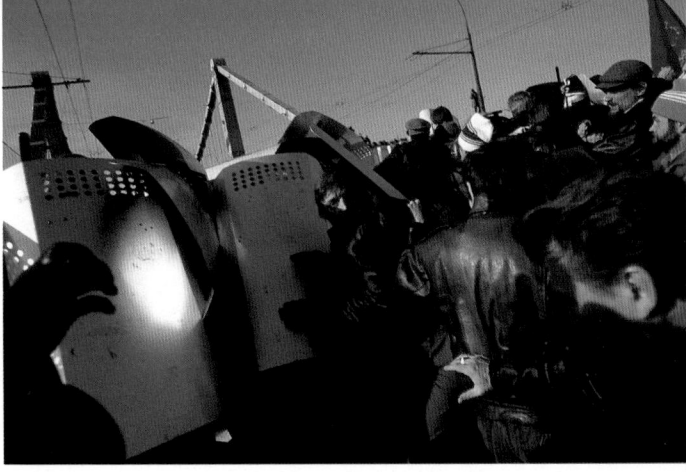

CHRISTOPHER MORRIS
Black Star for
Time Magazine,
USA

**FIRST PRIZE
STORIES**

9407

9407 (story starts on p.20)
Although the army put an end to Moscow's uprising by taking the White House on October 4, groups of anti-Yeltsin hard-liners attacking riot police continued to roam the Russian capital for days. Waving red flags, they raced through the streets long after most of the rebels had surrendered.

Facing page: An injured friend is carried to safety. Bottom left: Soldiers caught in the cross-fire near the parliament building, where uncaptured snipers continued their attacks. When the dust settled, the death count stood at almost 150, with about 1,000 people seriously injured.

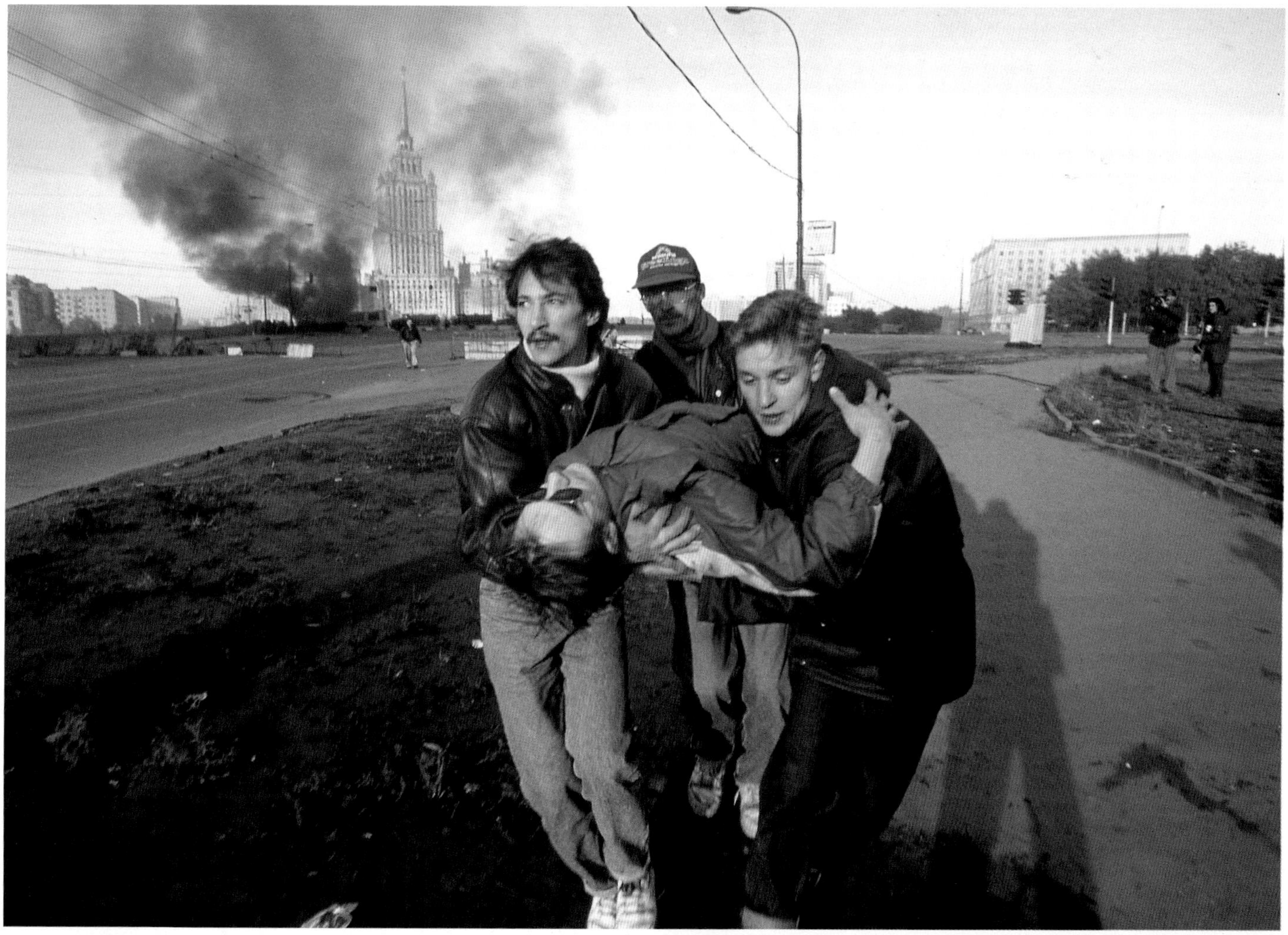

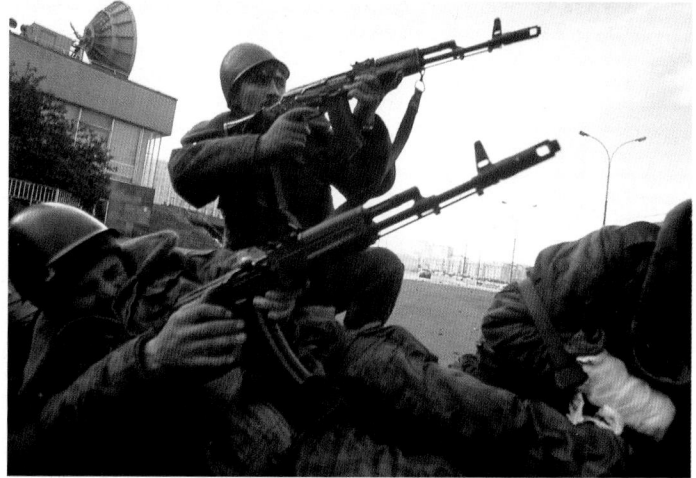

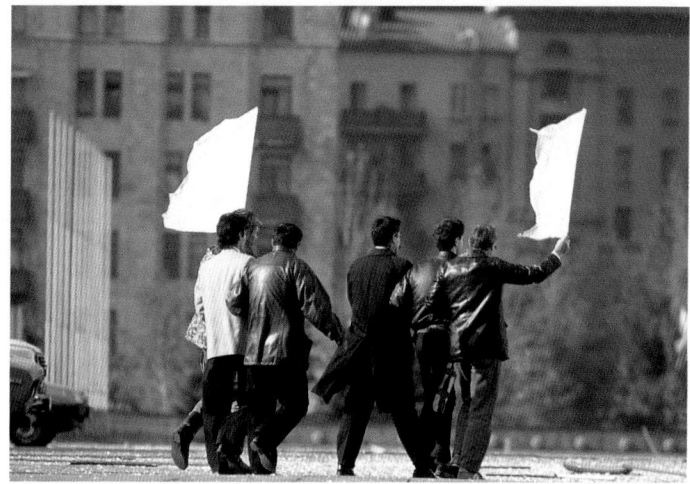

RON RICHARDS
UK,
Gamma Liaison,
USA

**THIRD PRIZE
STORIES**

9408

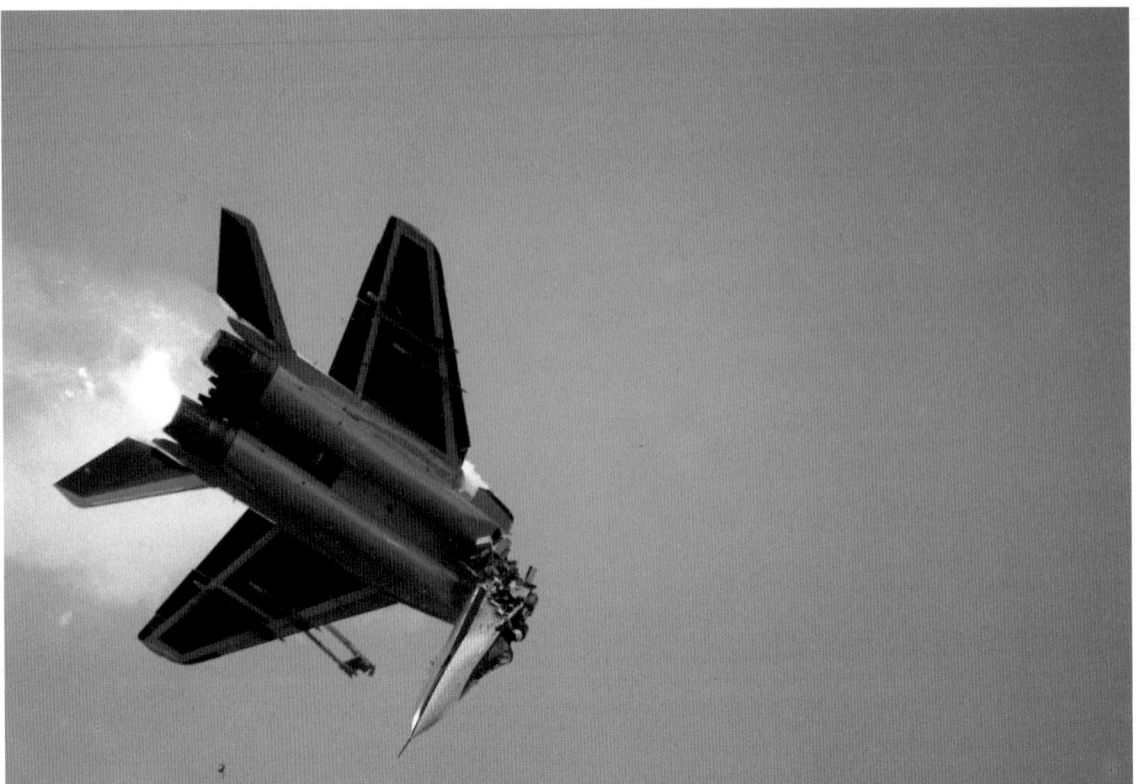

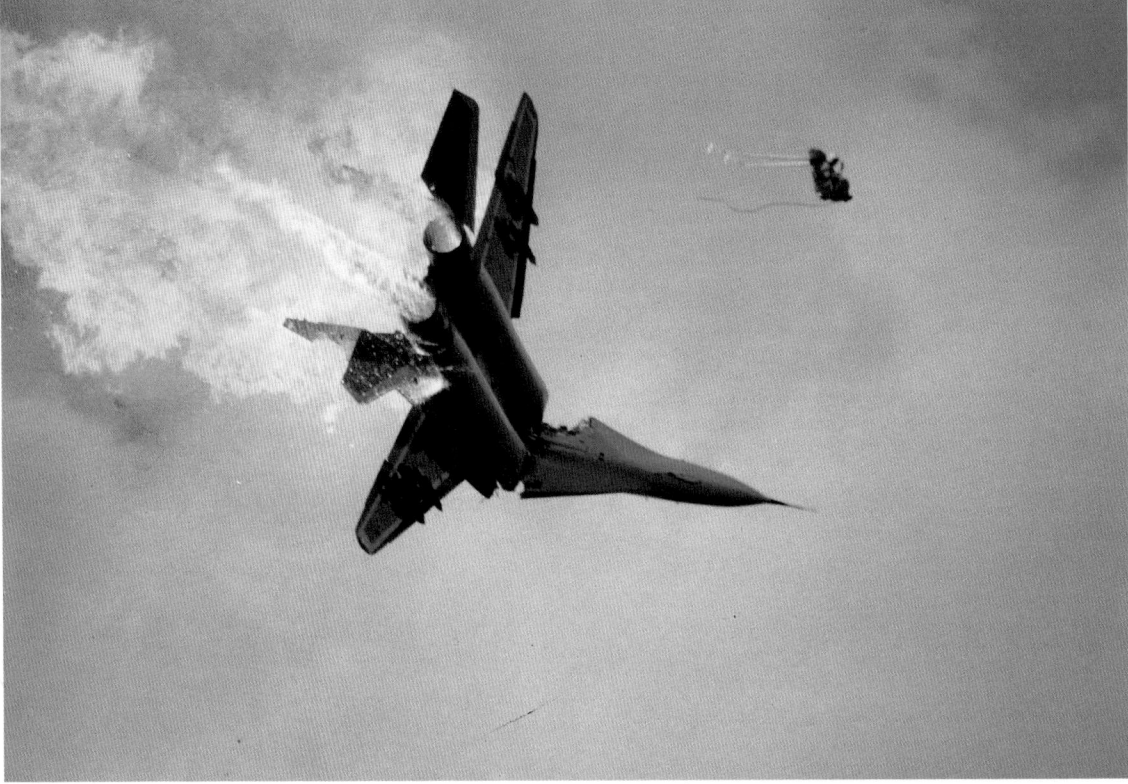

9408
Unscheduled event at the 1993 International
Air Tattoo in Fairford, England. During an
aerobatics display two Russian MiG-29 jet-
fighters collided, bending the fuselage of the
fighter shown above at cockpit level (top). The
second picture shows the other pilot ejecting
as his plane spirals to the ground in flames.
Both pilots escaped unharmed.

PAUL WATSON
Toronto Star,
Canada

**HONORABLE
MENTION
SINGLES**

9409

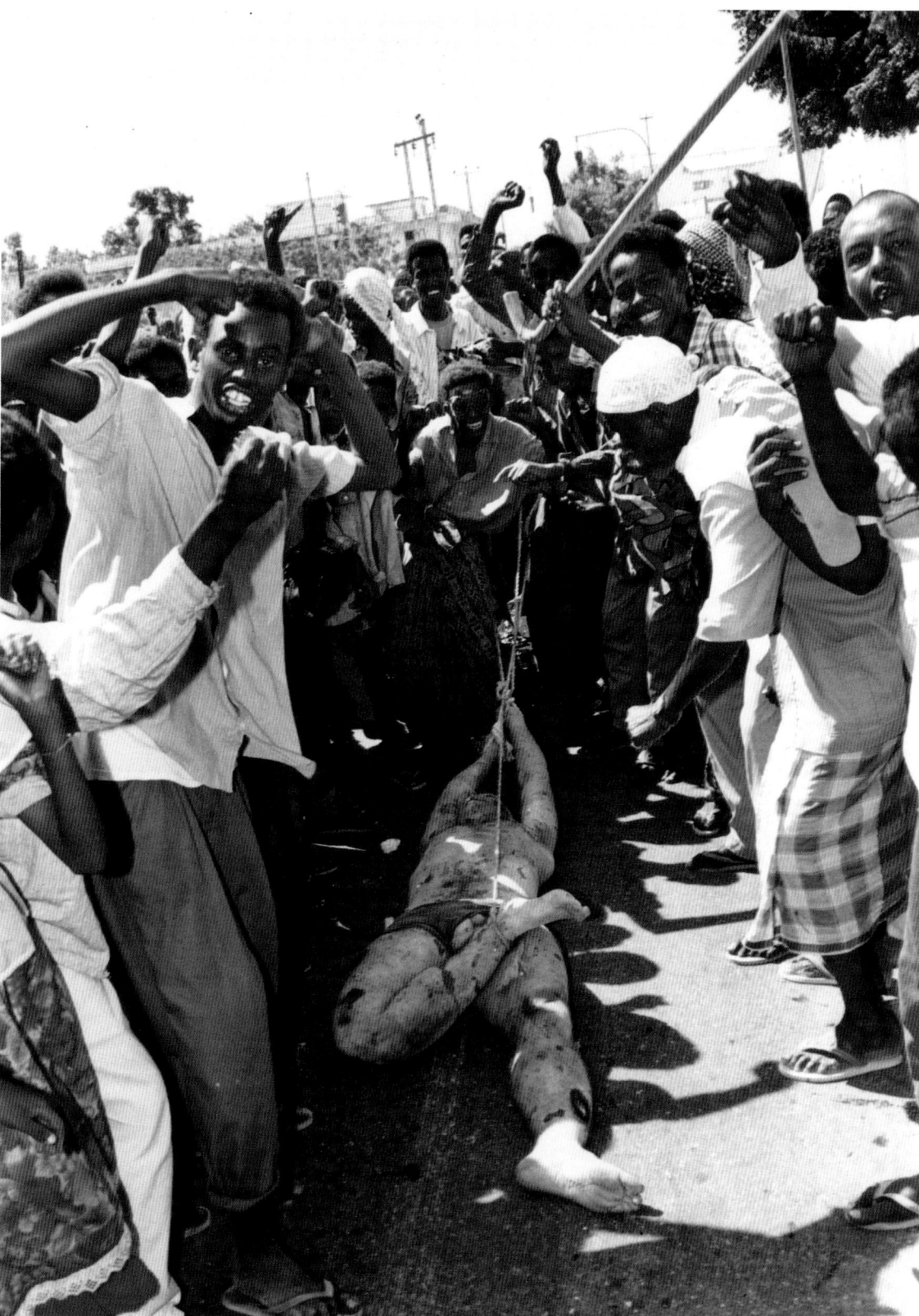

9409
Begun as a mission to relieve the famine in
December 1992, the American and UN pres-
ence in Somalia was increasingly the focus of
violent events. Negotiations with local war-
lords did not improve the situation, and the
foreign soldiers were often treated as invad-
ers. Here followers of General Aidid drag a
slain American through the streets of
Mogadishu.

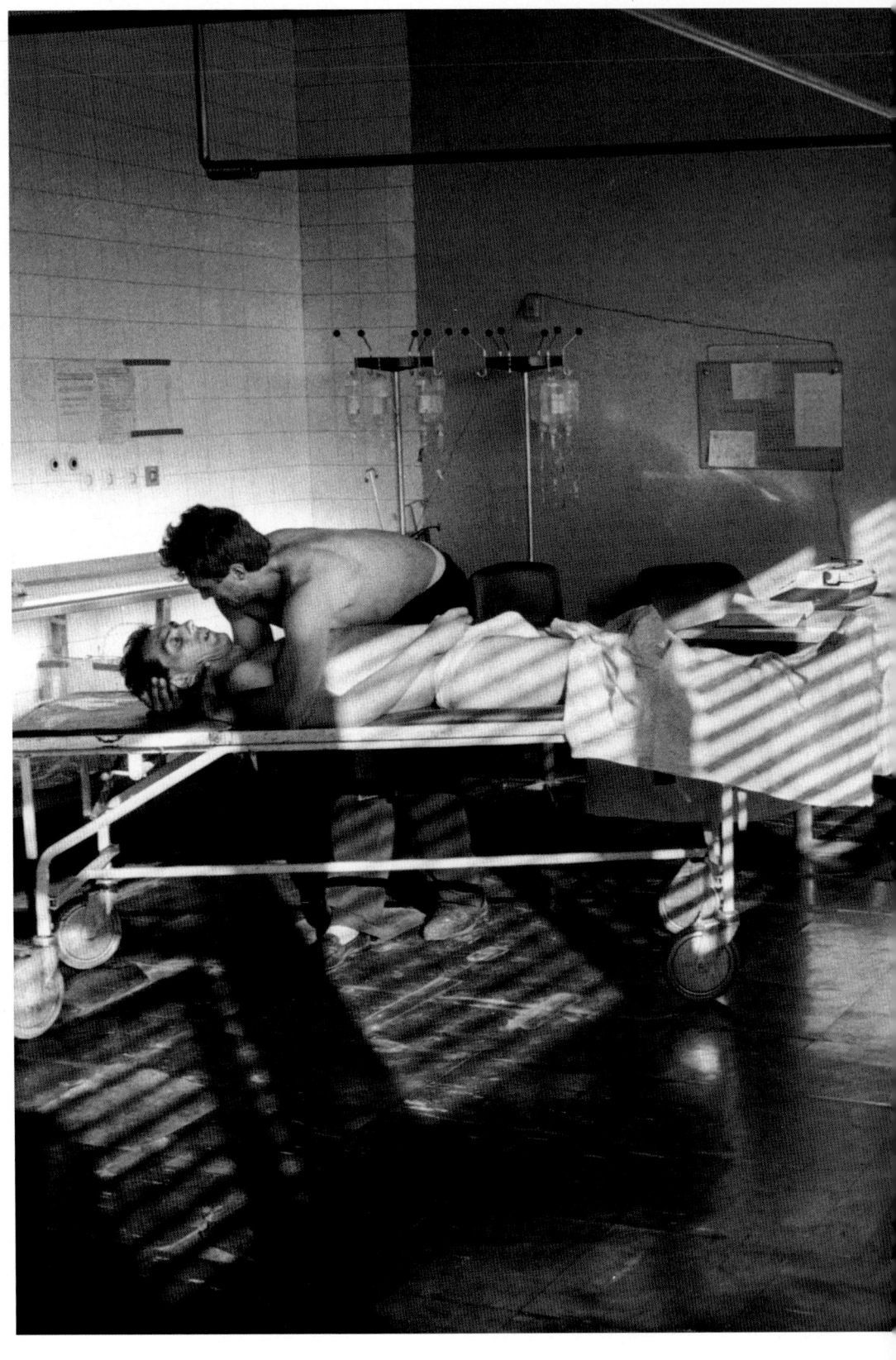

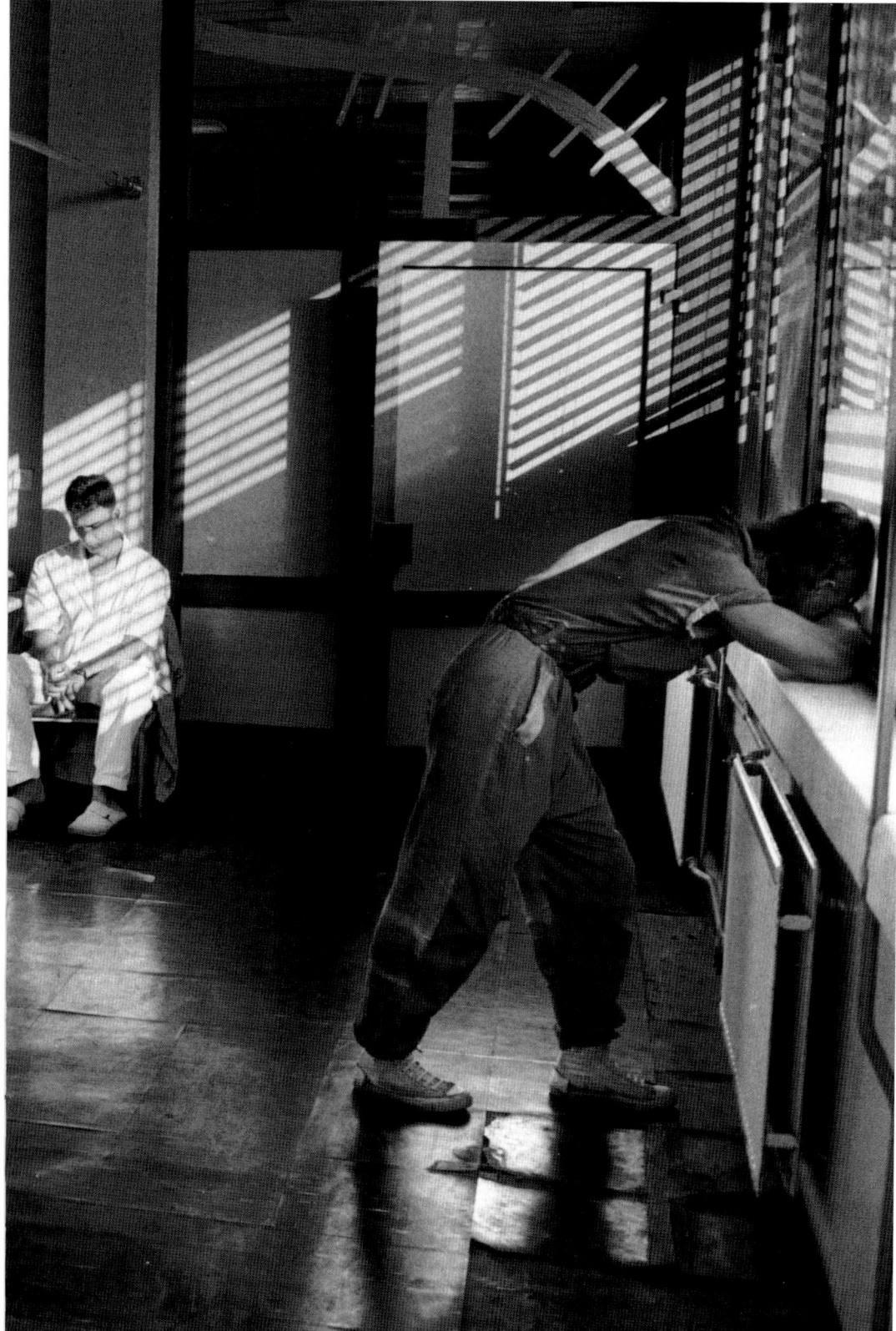

LUC DELAHAYE
France,
Sipa Press for
Newsweek Magazine,
USA

**FIRST PRIZE
SINGLES**

9410

9410
In July, Bosnian soldier Remzija Aljukic was shot by a Serb sniper near the center of Sarajevo. His brothers, who served in the same unit, rushed him to nearby Kosevo Hospital, a front-line medical center with only the most basic facilities. He died a few minutes after arriving at the emergency ward.

Just as the doctors give up trying to revive Remzija, his brothers burst into the room. With just one medic remaining, they succumb to their desperate, impotent grief. At the time, between 15 and 30 war casualties died at Kosevo Hospital every day.

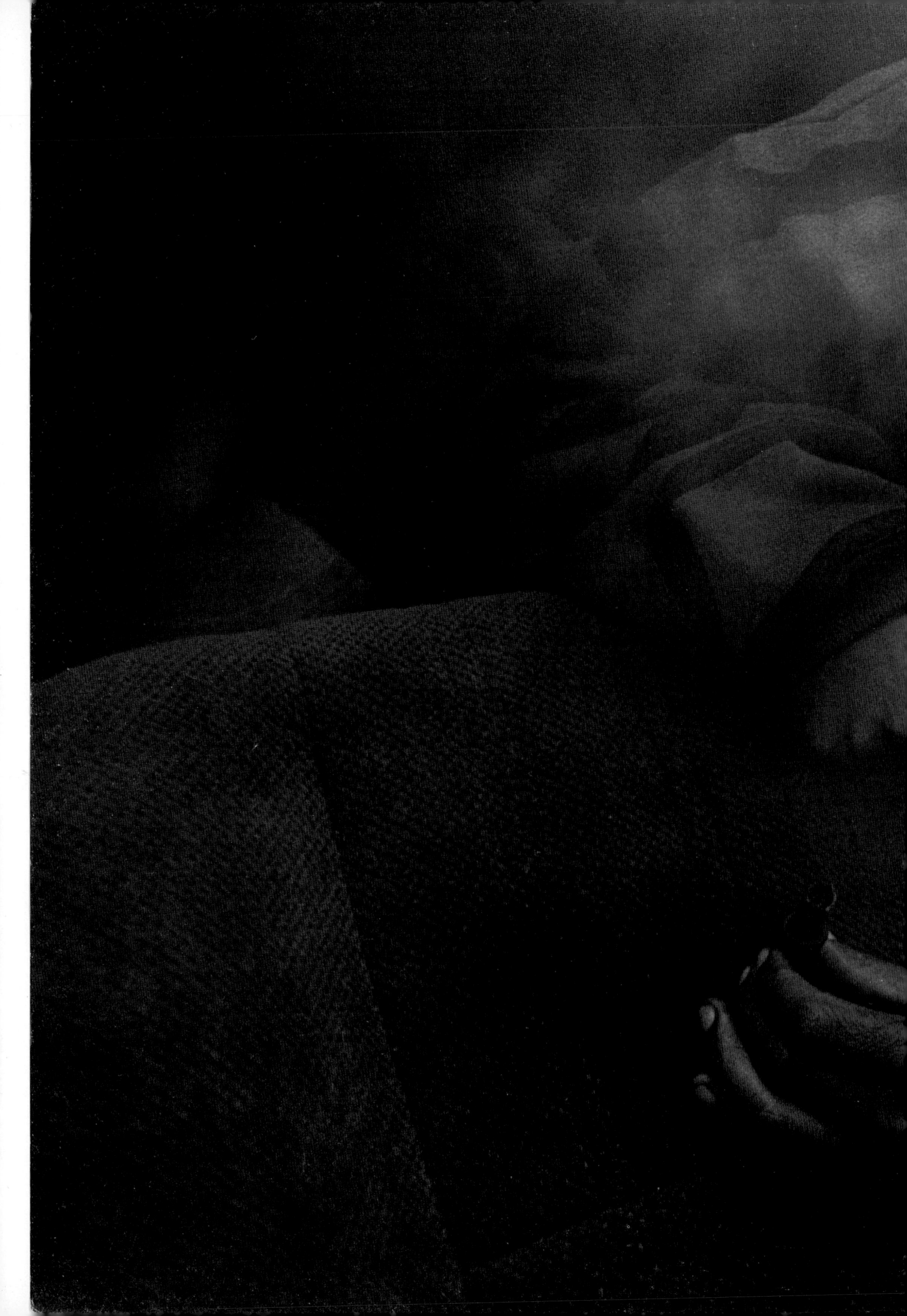

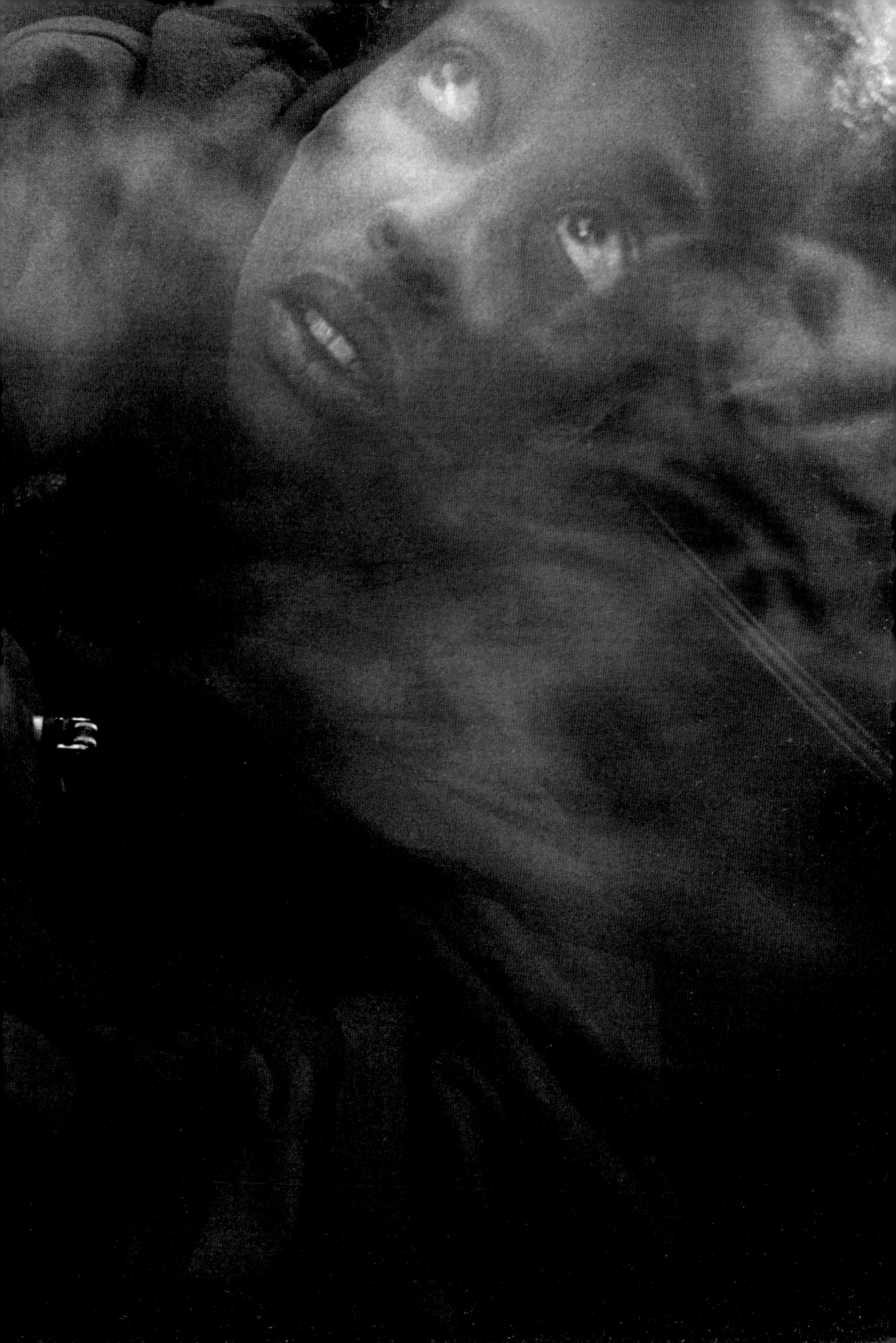

STANLEY GREENE
USA,
Agence Vu,
France

**THIRD PRIZE
SINGLES**

9412

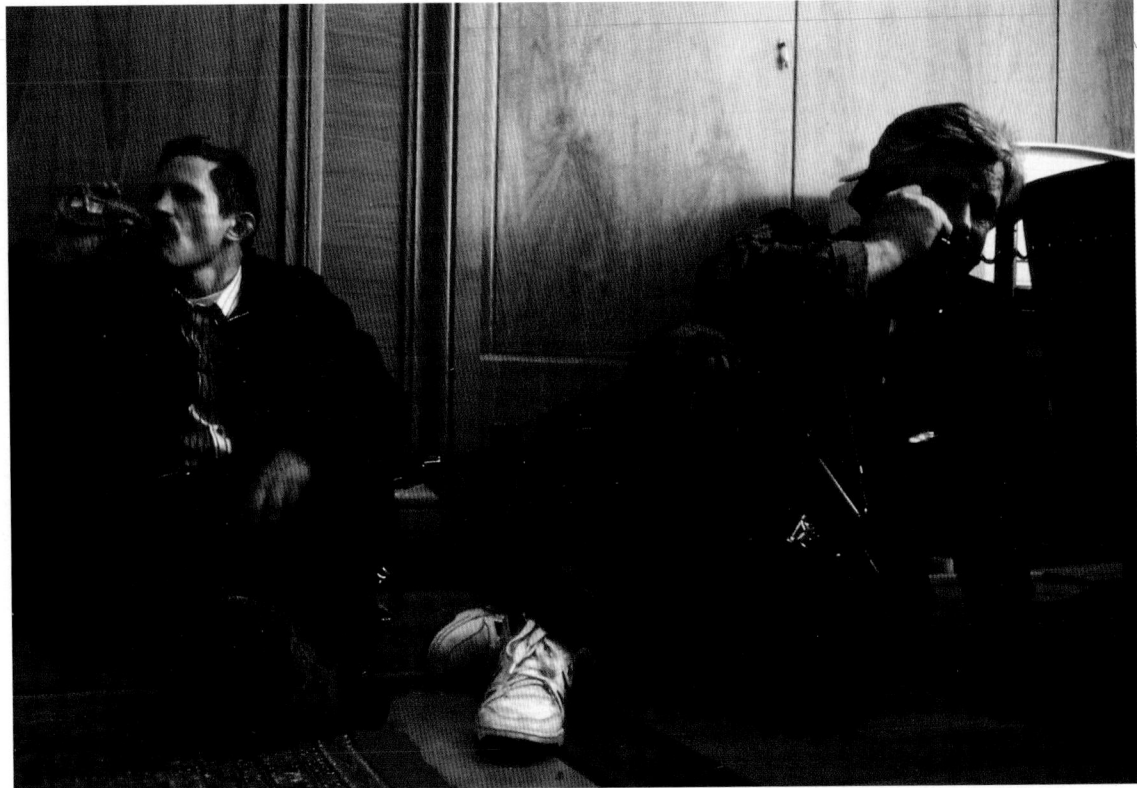

RICHARD ELLIS
Reuters
News Pictures,
UK

9413

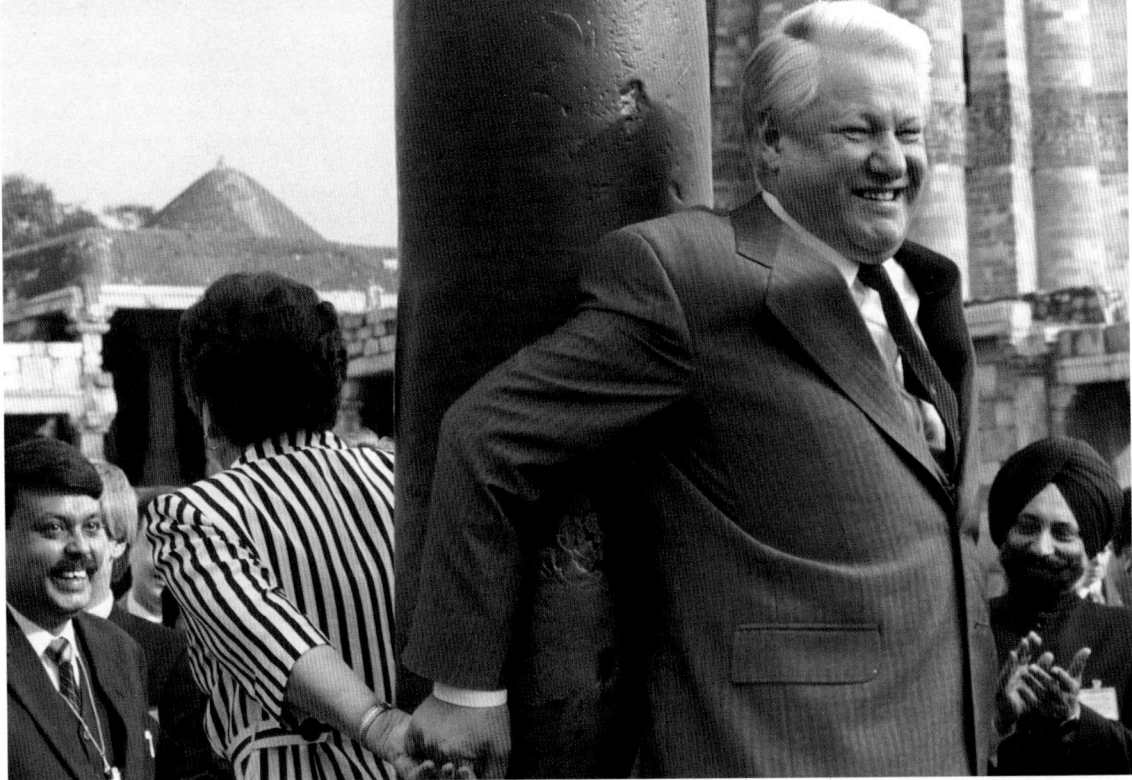

9412
Dressed in combat fatigues, former Russian
Vice President Alexandr Rutskoi cowers with
his bodyguard on the floor of the White
House, Moscow's parliament building. When
Rutskoi's diverse following tried to seize
power in early October, Yeltsin quashed the
rebellion by sending in tanks.

9413
On a visit to New Delhi, India, Russian
President Boris Yeltsin clasps the hands of
his wife Niana around an 800-year-old iron
pillar. Legend has it that for a year fortune will
smile upon those who link hands in this way.

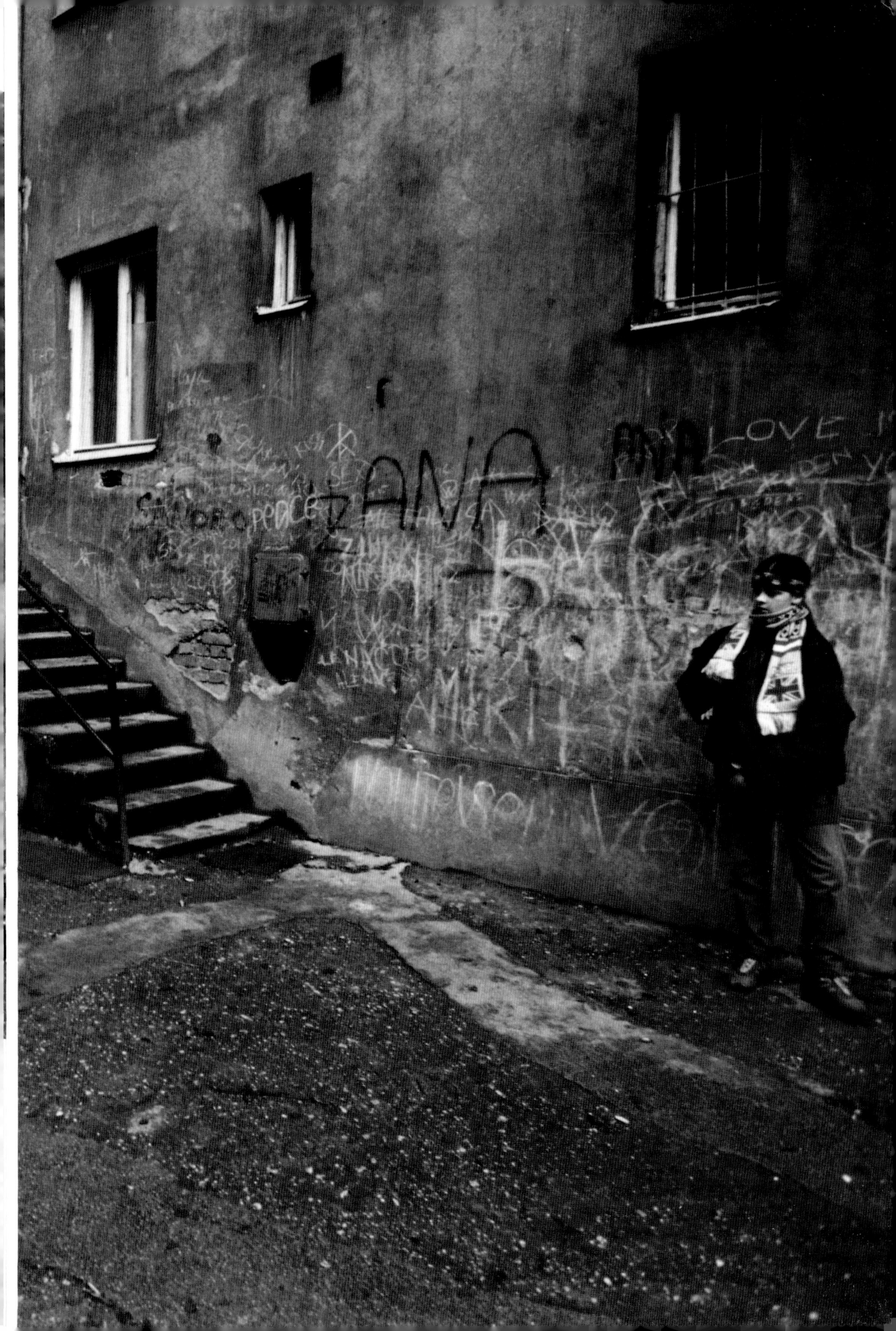

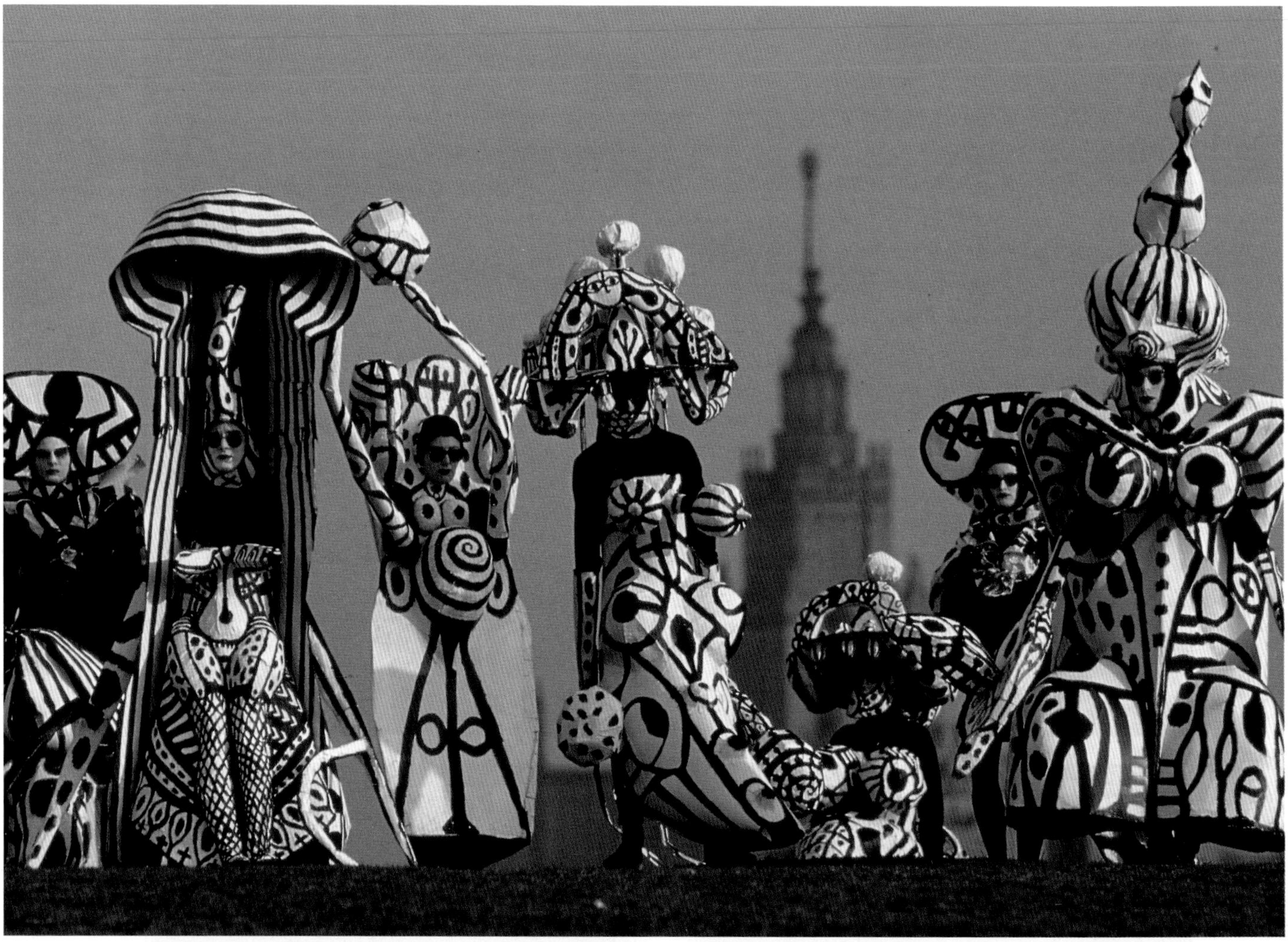

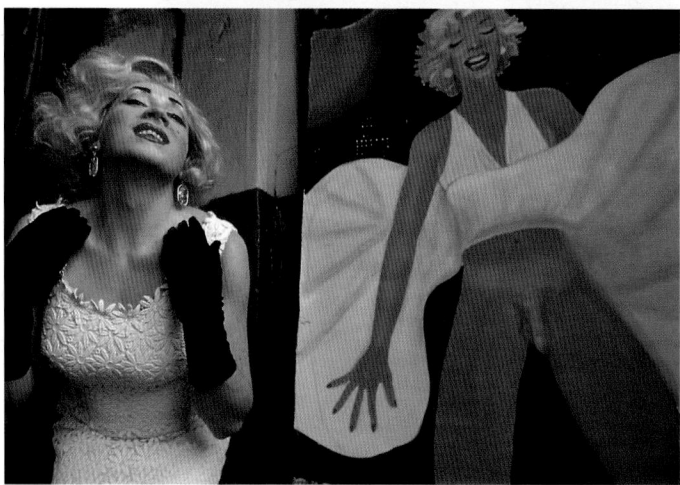

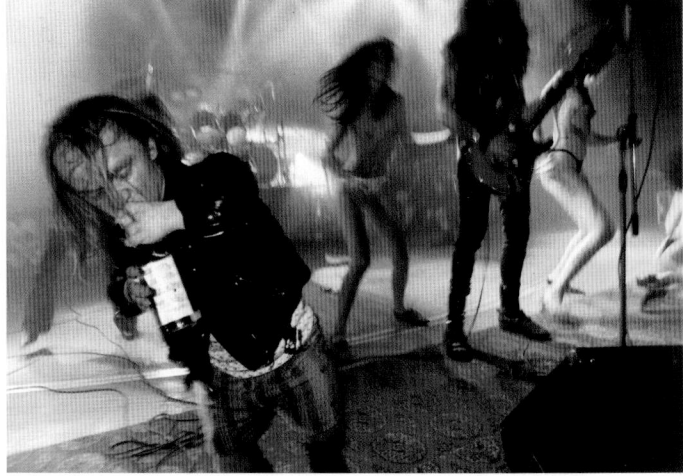

HANS-JÜRGEN BURKARD
Bilderberg for Stern Magazine, Germany

THIRD PRIZE STORIES

9418

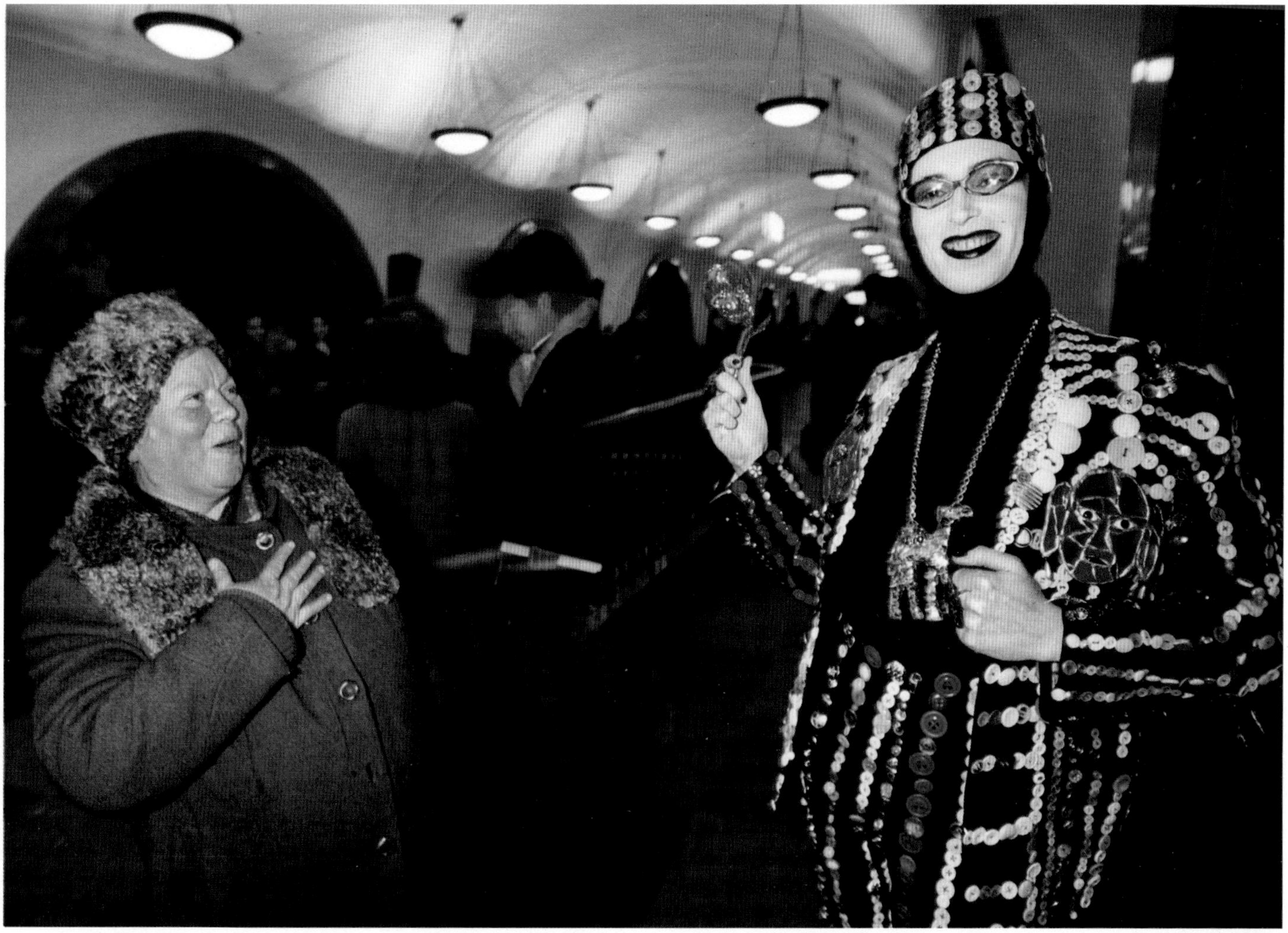

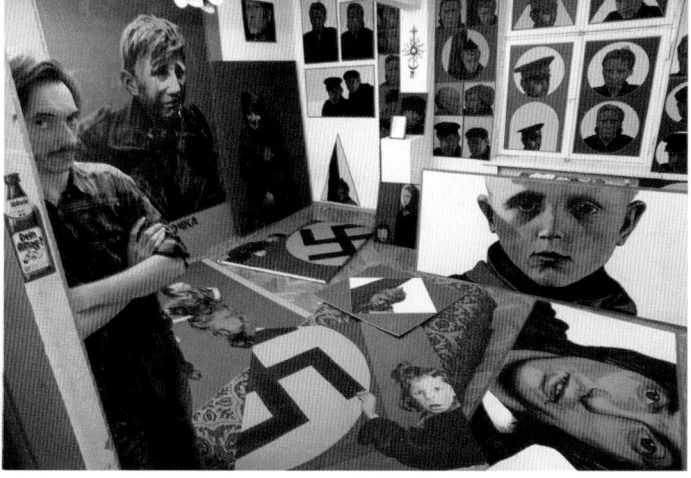

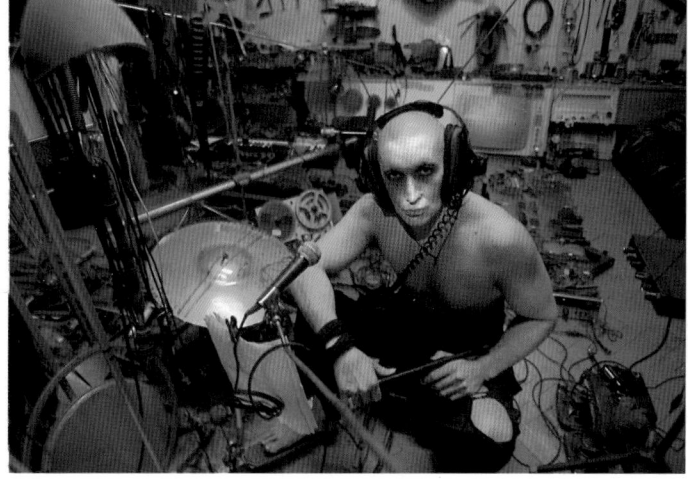

9418
Moscow's young artists refer to themselves as 'the children of the perestroika'. They have their own way of channeling their creative energy – and of having a good time. Top left: Fashion designer Andrei Bartenev hides behind one of his startling designs, executed in papier-mâché. Top: The same designer models one of his creations in the Moscow metro.

Facing page, bottom: Vladislav Mamyshev, also known as Monroe, with self-portrait. Heavy metal group Corosia Metalla features a midget in a mask and nude dancers. Above: War and dictatorship are Dmitriy Vrubel's favorite subjects. His one-room apartment doubles as a studio. Blue light creates an underwater atmosphere in technophile Alyosha Tegin's abode.

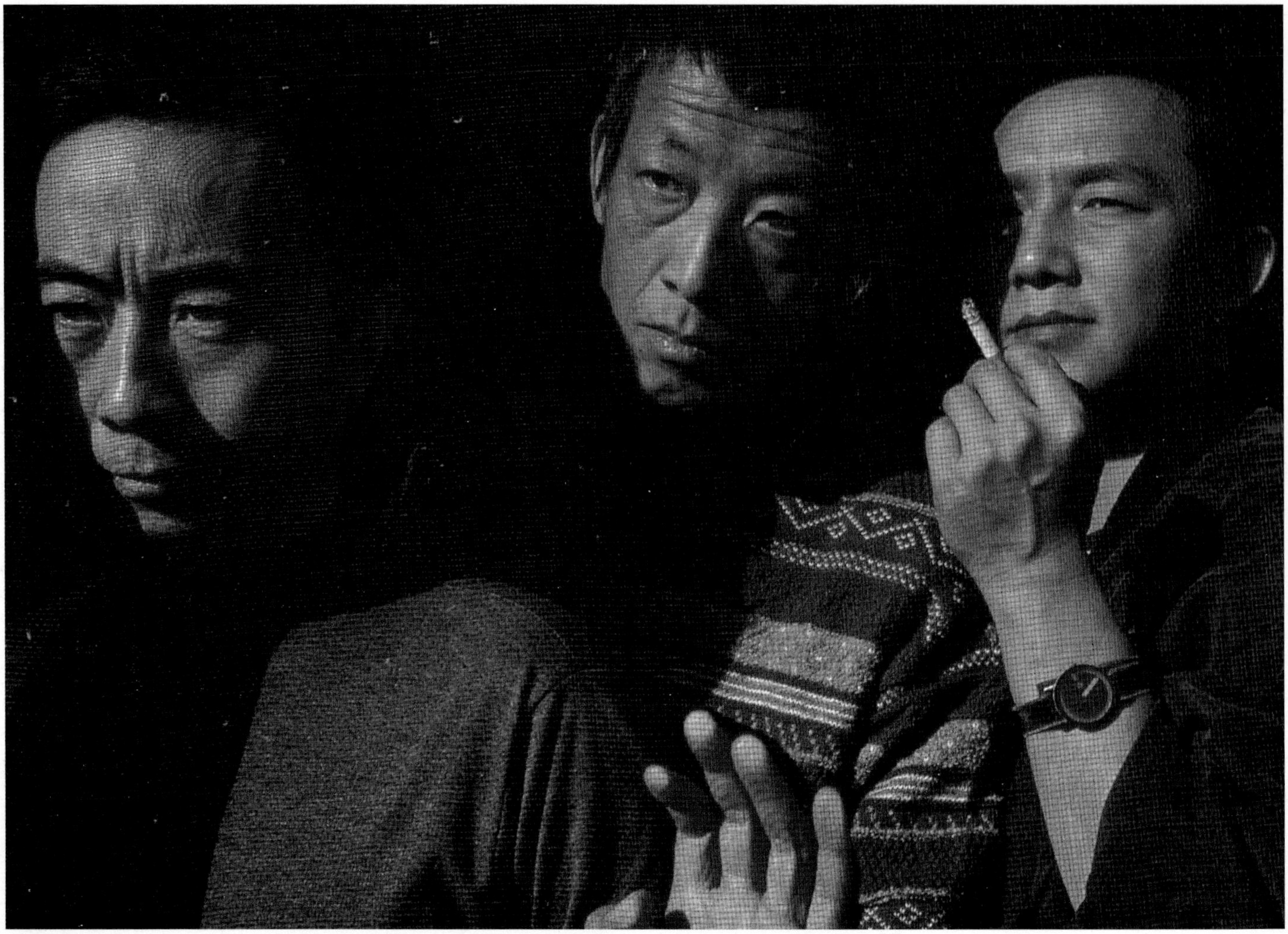

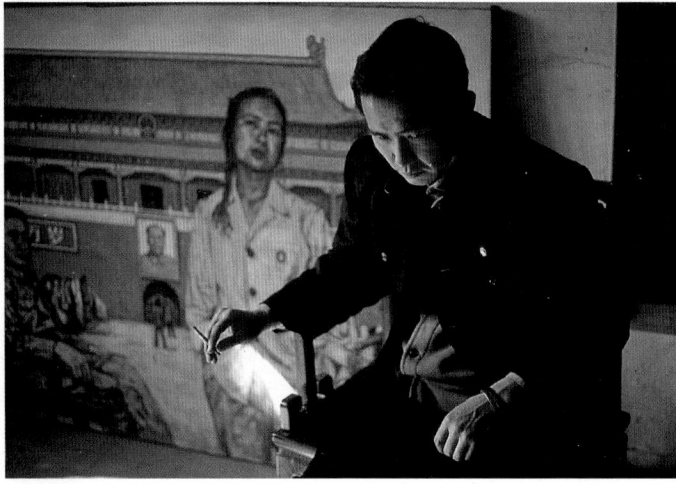
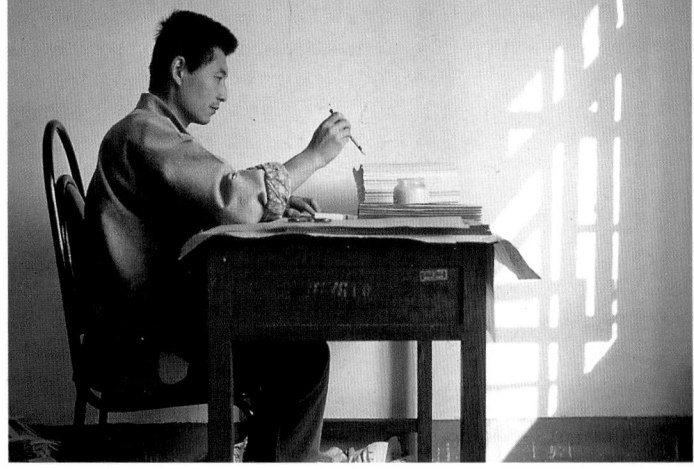

GUEORGUI PINKHASSOV
Russia,
Magnum Photos
for New York Times
Magazine,
USA

FIRST PRIZE STORIES

9419

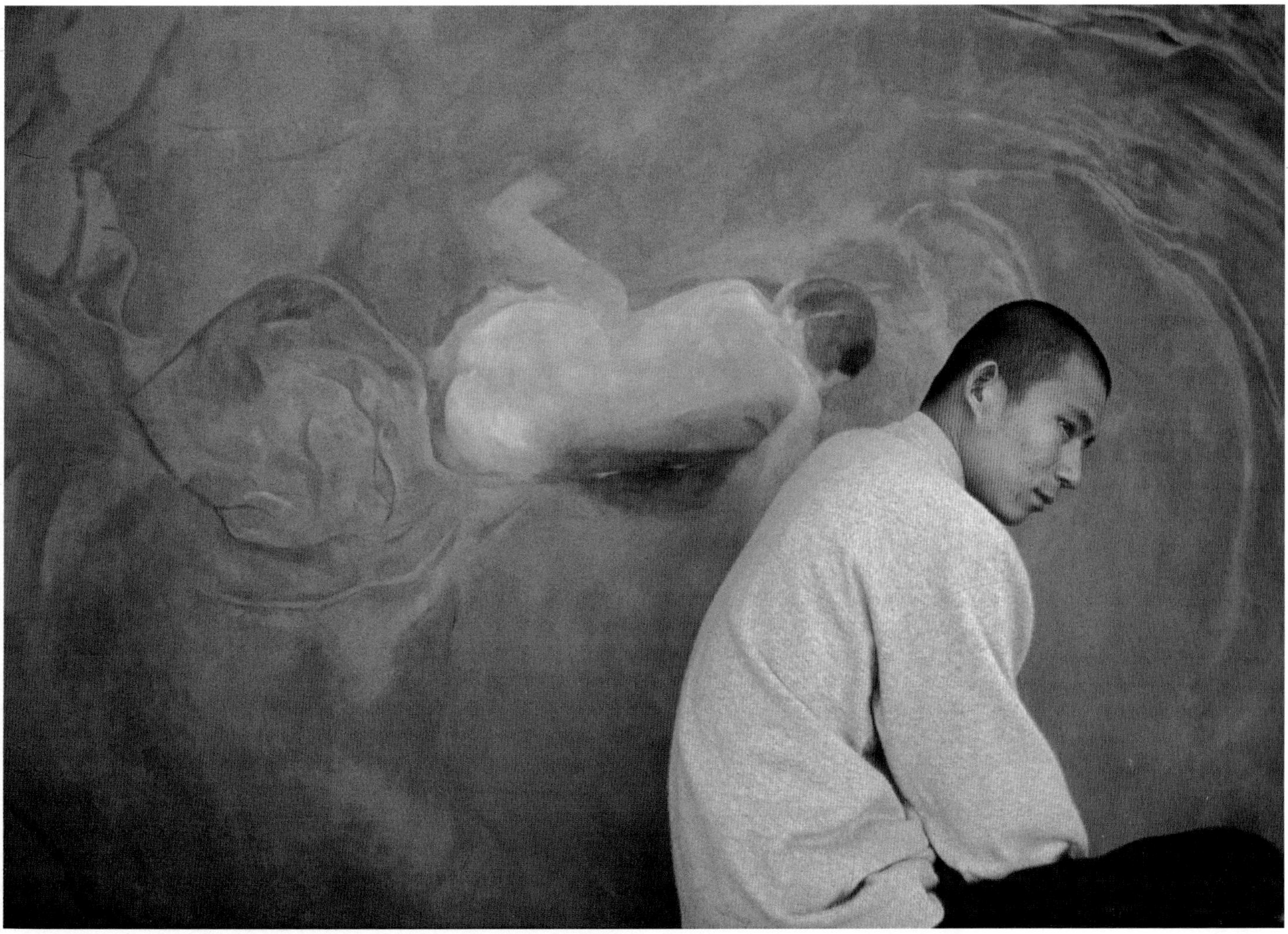

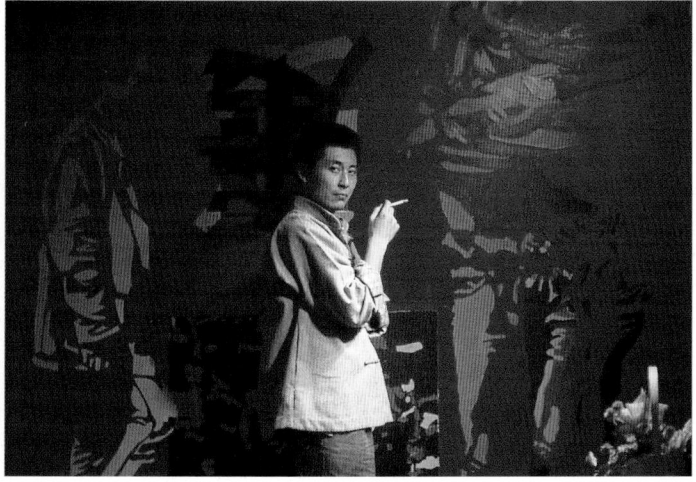
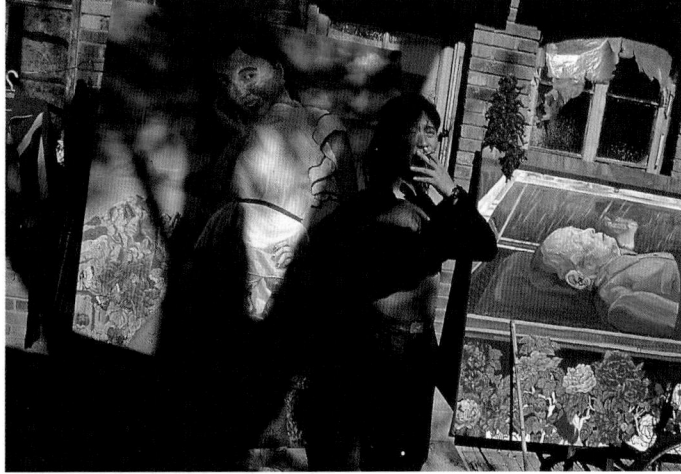

9419
Groups of Chinese artists pitch their irony and humor against the intransigence of the communist regime. Exhibitions of little political significance have been closed down more than once, while gestures of defiance are often so subtle as to go unnoticed abroad. Cynical Realism and Political Pop are two of the movements in the Chinese avant-garde.

The three men at top left belong to a group known as the New Analysts. Fang Lijun (top) paints characters exuding a sense of complete purposelessness. Bottom, from left: Yang Yipin places young people in Tiananmen Square. Geng Jianyi and Zhang Peili live and work in the lake-side city of Hangzhou, and Liu Wei is an exponent of the post-'89 Cynical Realists.

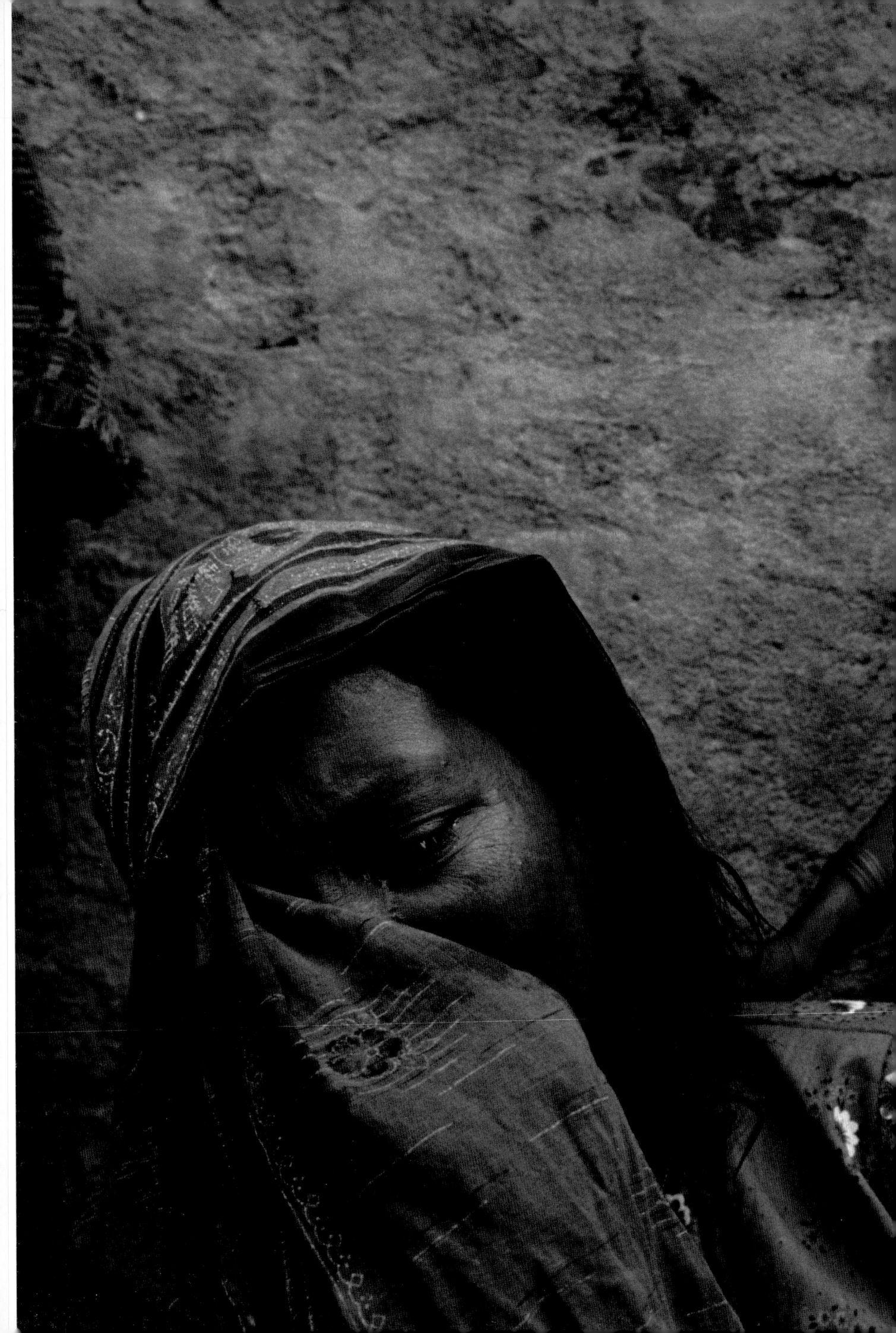

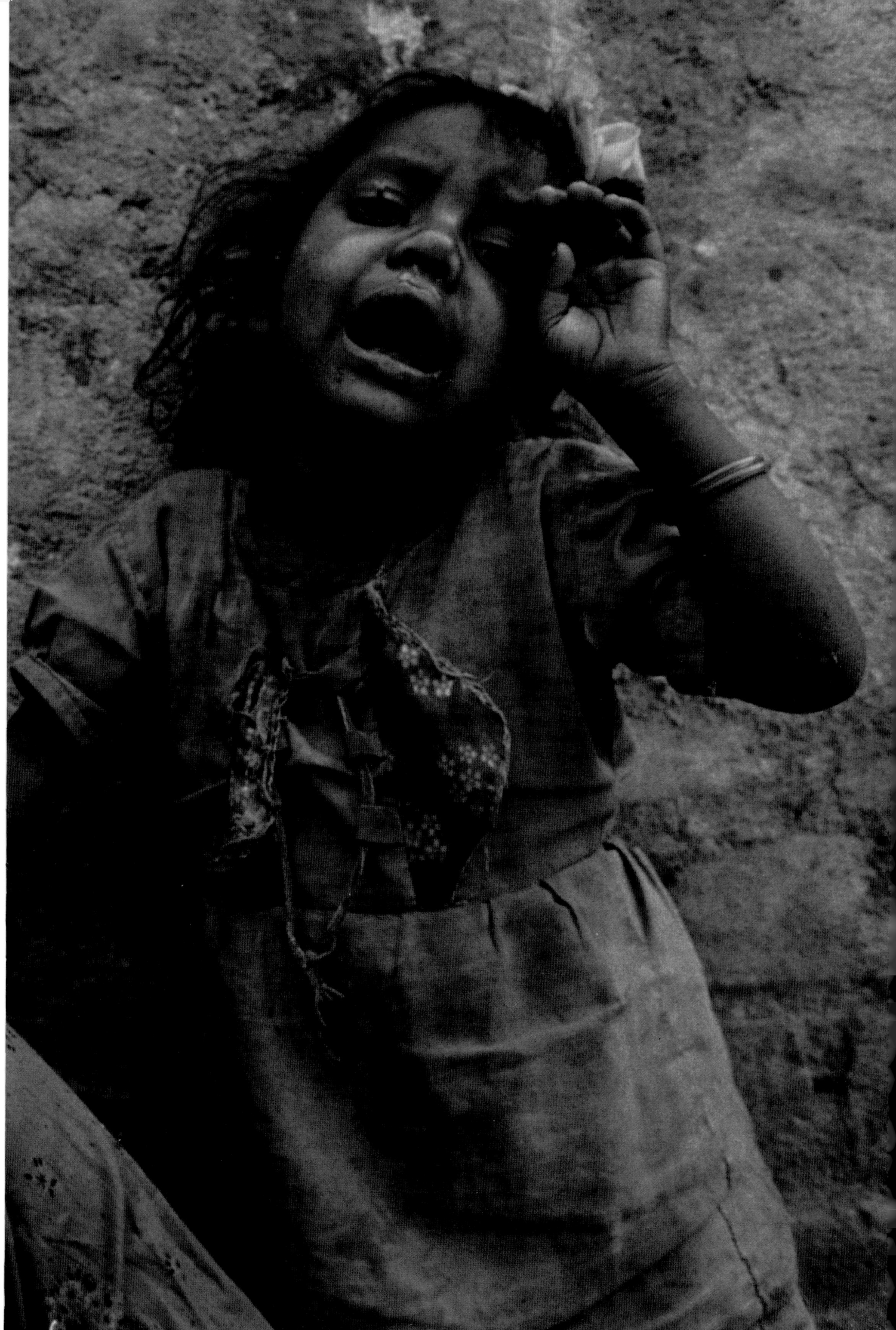

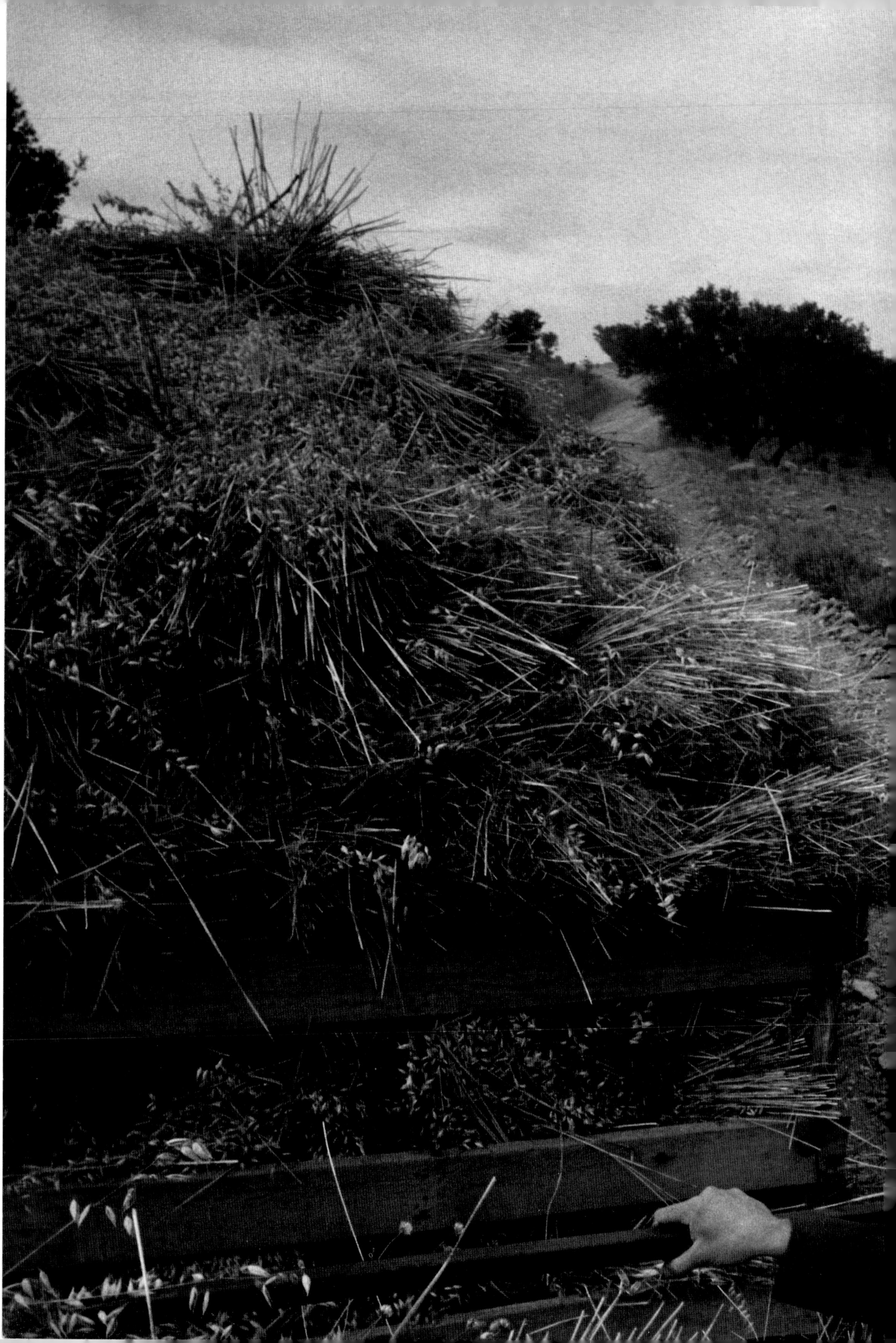

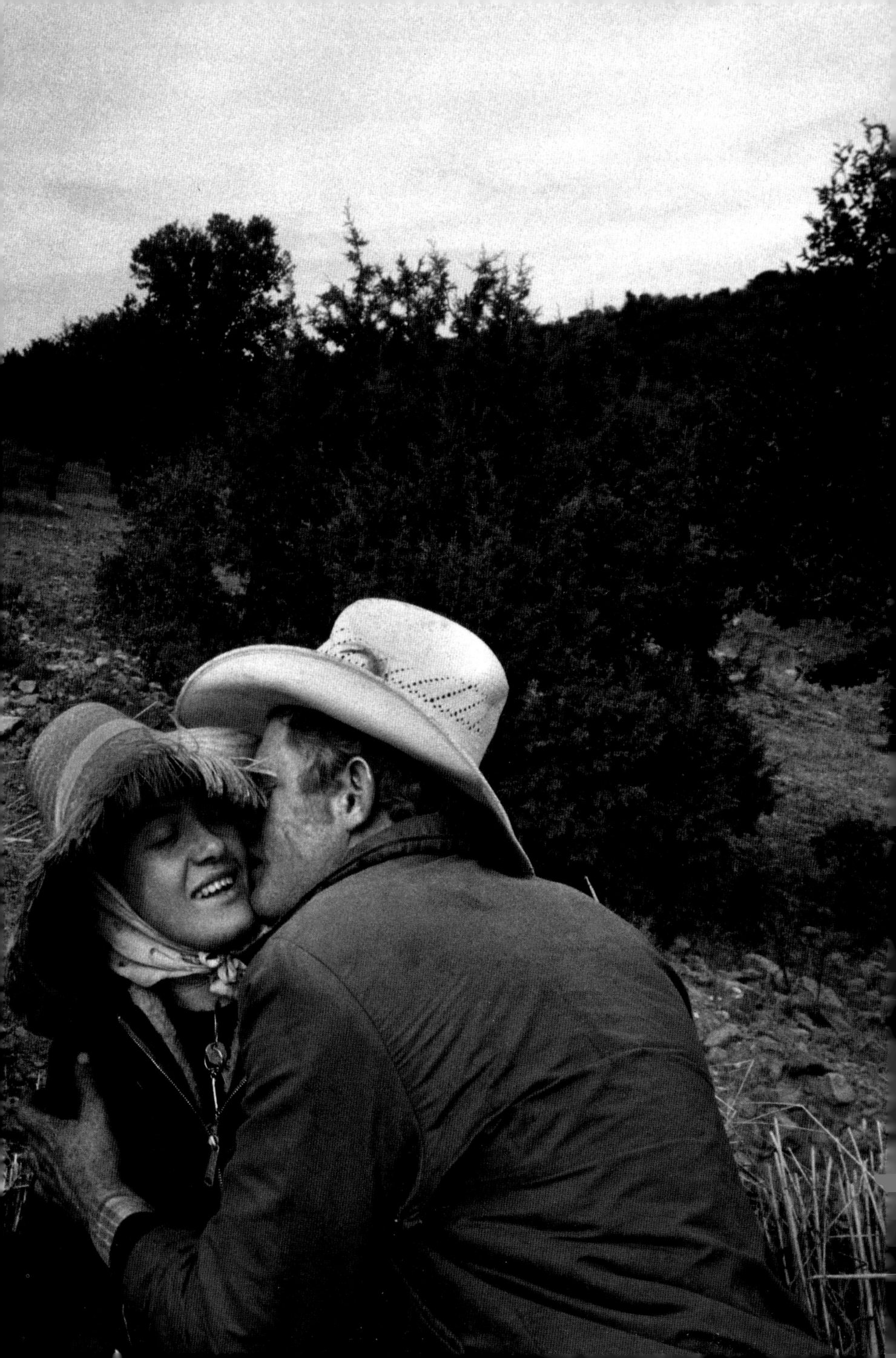

LARRY TOWELL
Canada,
Magnum Photos,
USA

**FIRST PRIZE
STORIES**

9427

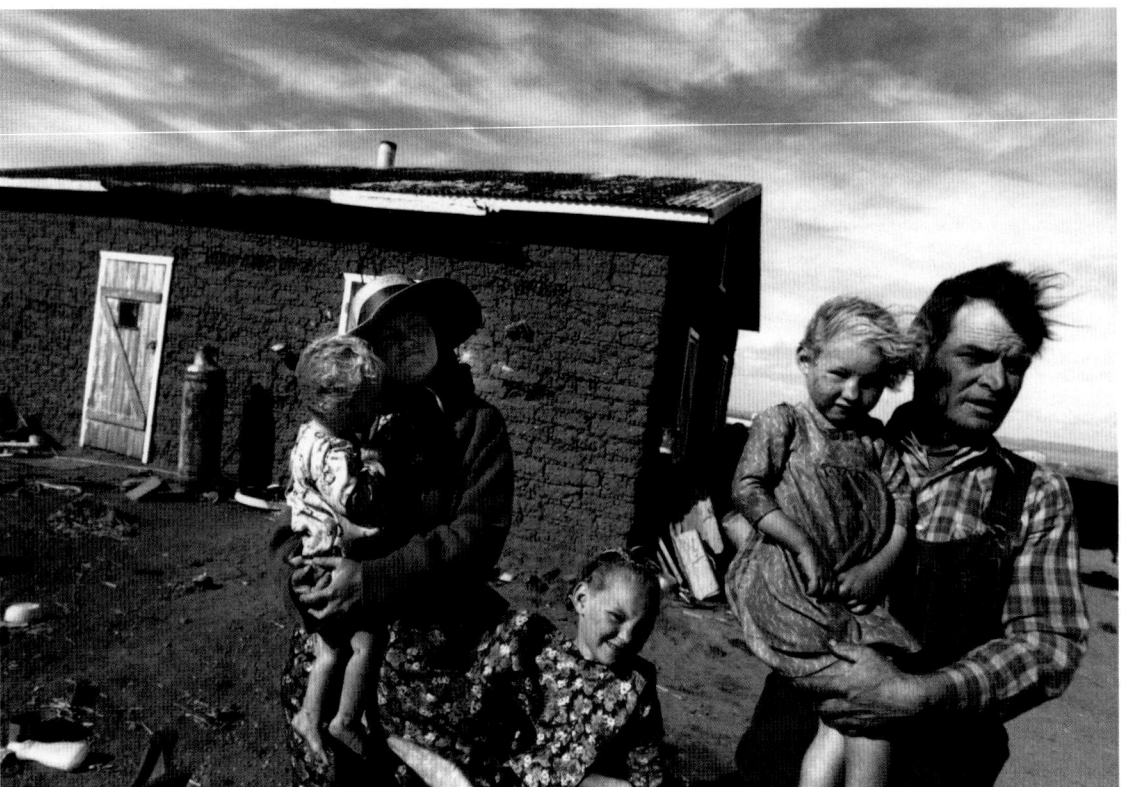

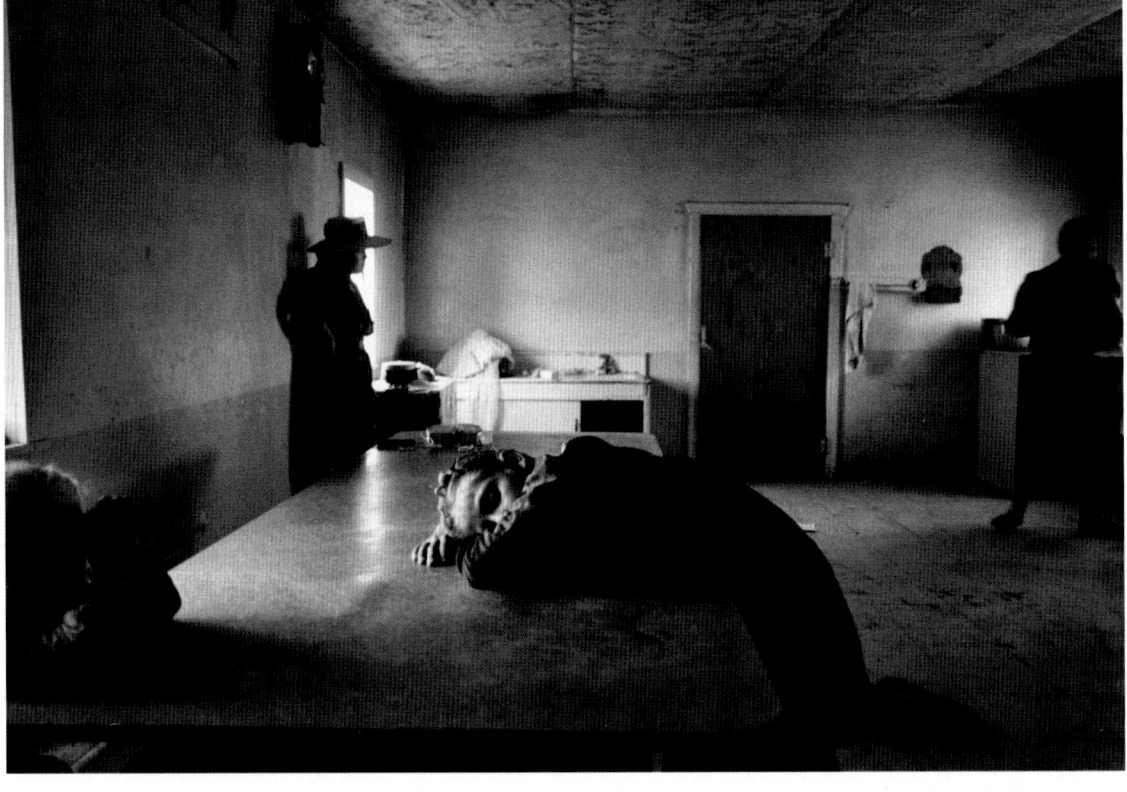

9427 (story starts on p.58)
This story has the Mennonites, a protestant group descended from the 16th-century Anabaptists, as its subject. Founded in the Netherlands, the Mennonites oppose military service and favor plain dress. They believe that schooling threatens their way of life. The photographer, who lives in Canada, joined his Mennonite neighbors for a visit to relatives in Mexico.

Previous pages: Anita and Hornelio, a young married couple, embrace on a wagon full of sheaves gathered in the fields of Chihuahua, Mexico. Top: Outside their house in Casas Grandes, Herman Fehr, his wife and three daughters are almost blown off their feet by the strong wind. Above: Nine-year-old Anita Wall at her home in Las Botellas (story continues).

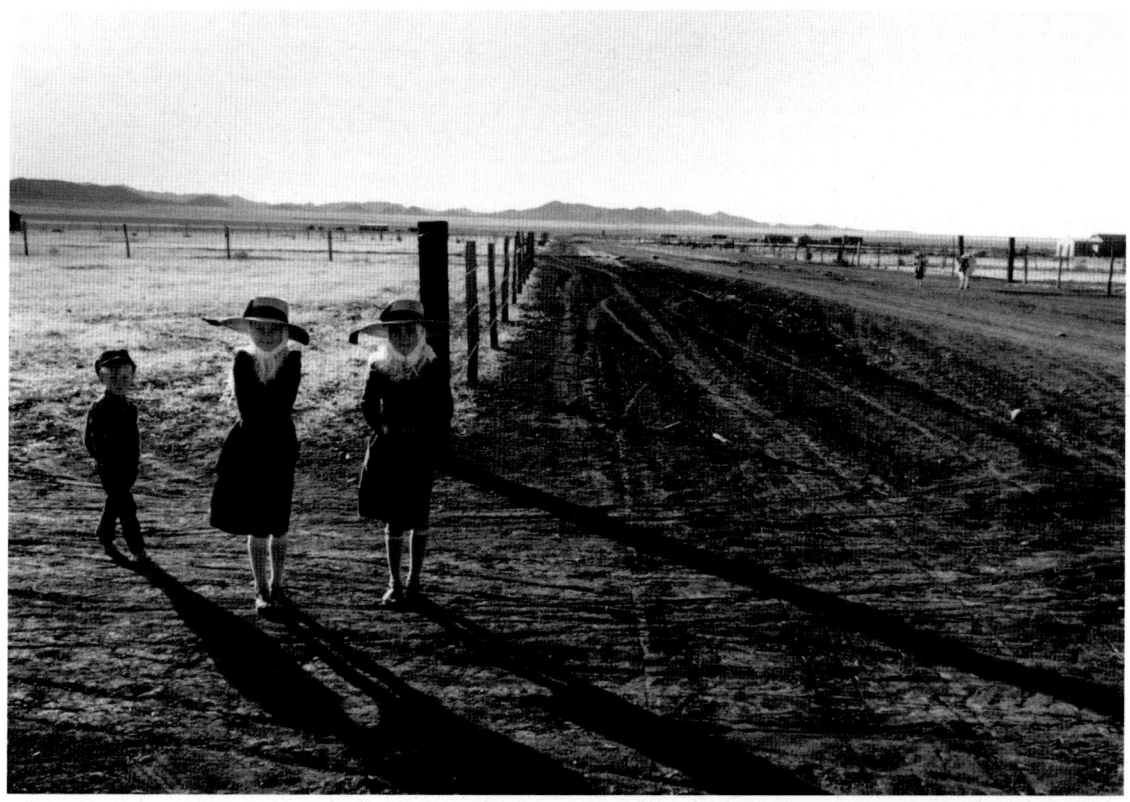

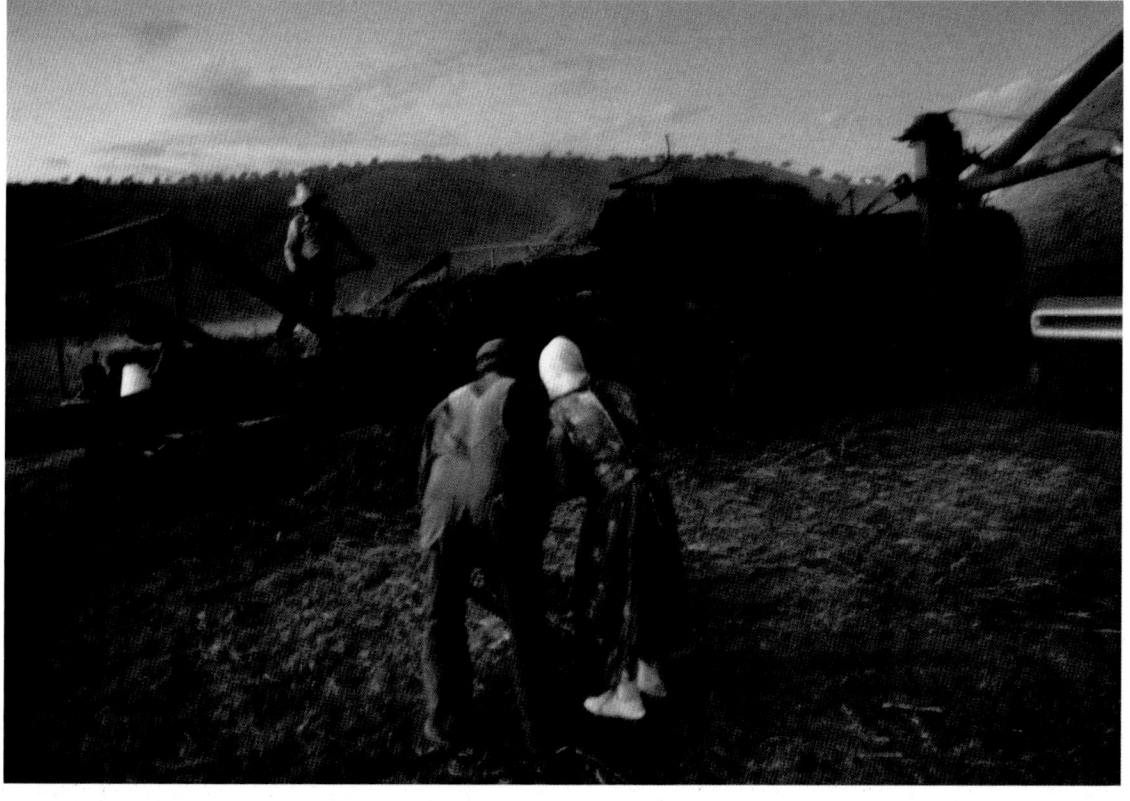

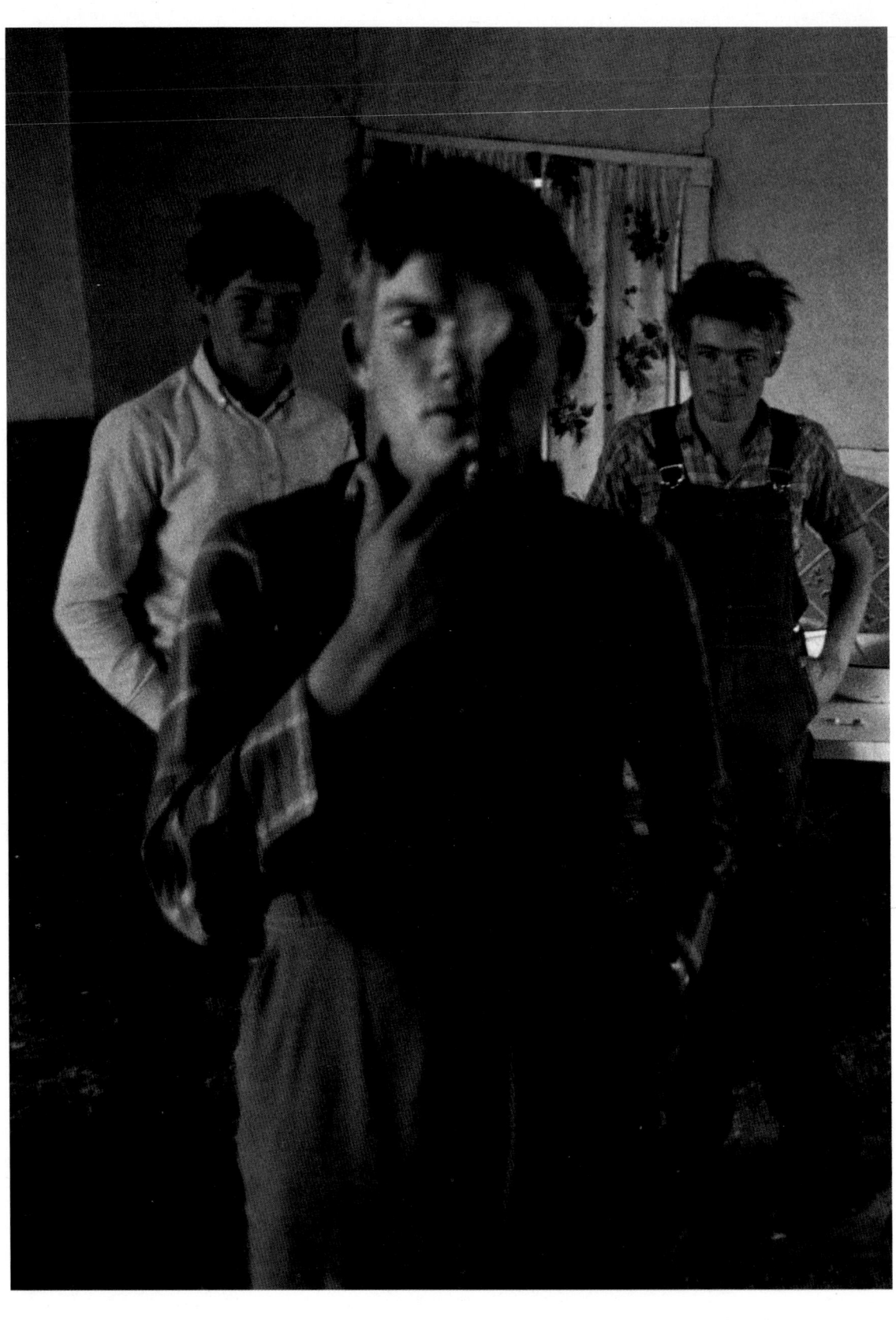

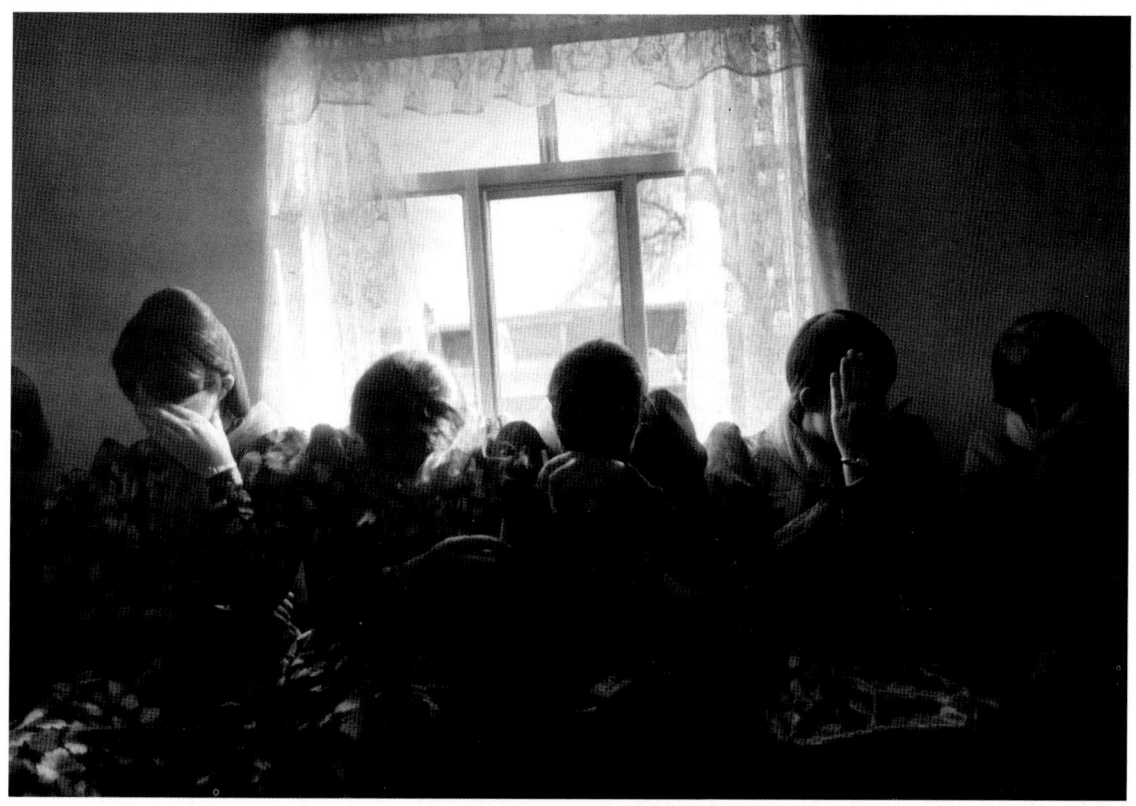

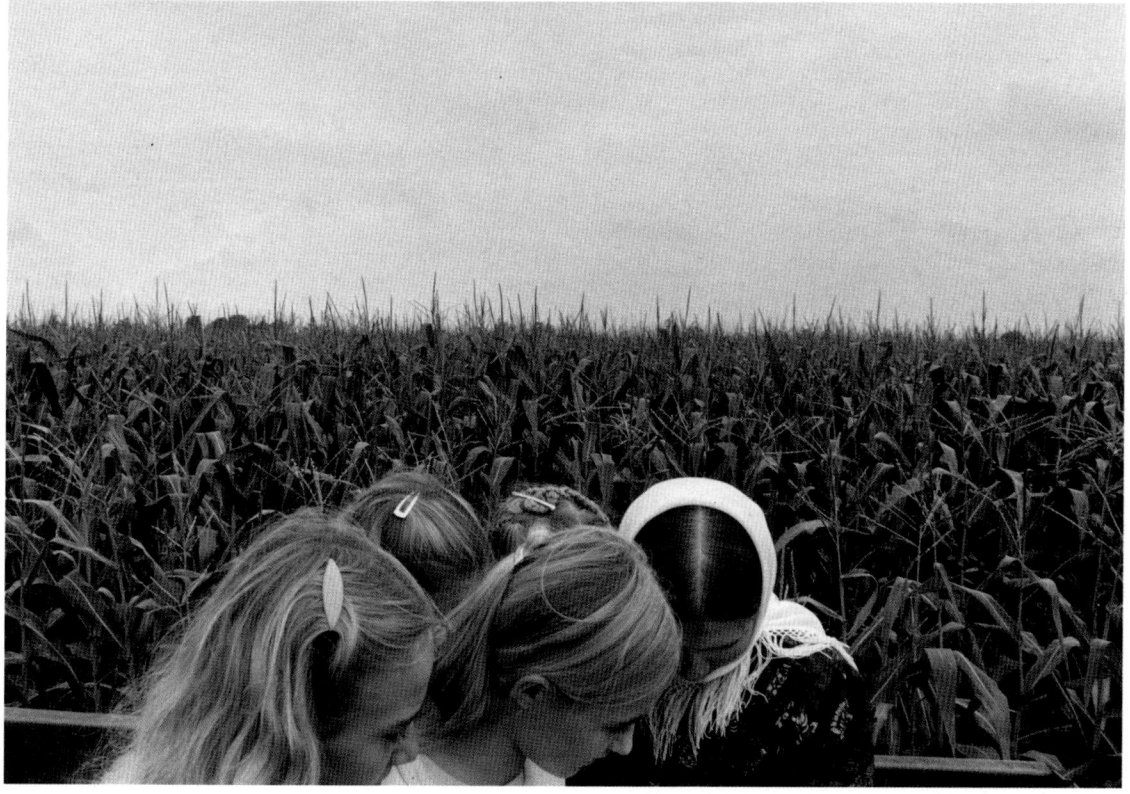

9427 (continued)
In the 1920s, groups of Mennonites emigrated from Canada to Mexico to escape government interference. Today some 50,000 of them still live in northern Mexico, but thousands have also moved back north because of the harsh conditions south of the border. In the Mexican desert, cattle often have to be fed cactus instead of grain.

In most Mexican colonies jewelry, watches and recorded music are banned, and it is forbidden to drive or own a vehicle. Those who return to the fertile fields of Canada (above), however, frequently have difficulty adjusting to a more sophisticated society. Next pages: Mennonite girls hurry home along the dusty, windswept roads of northern Mexico.

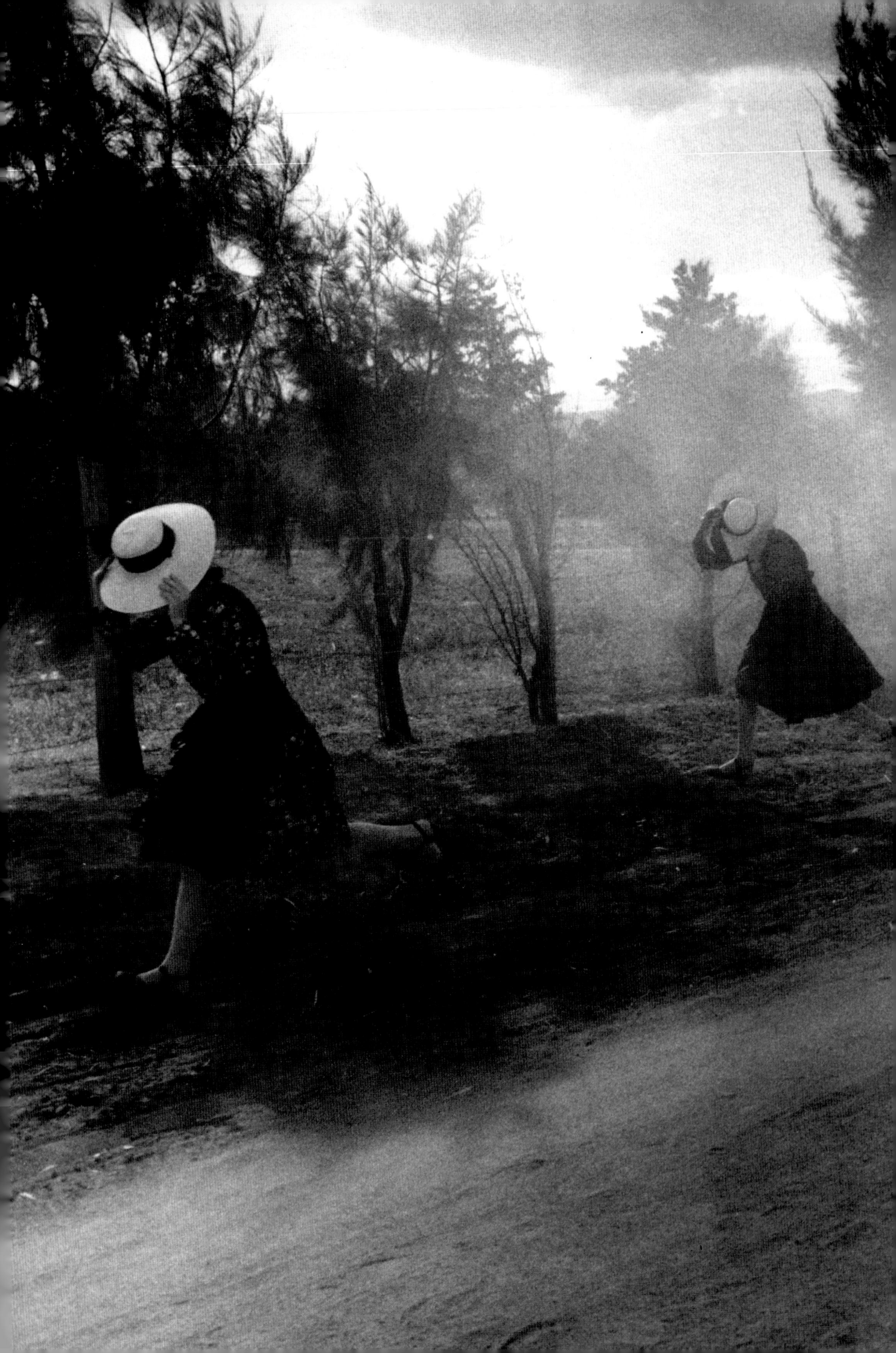

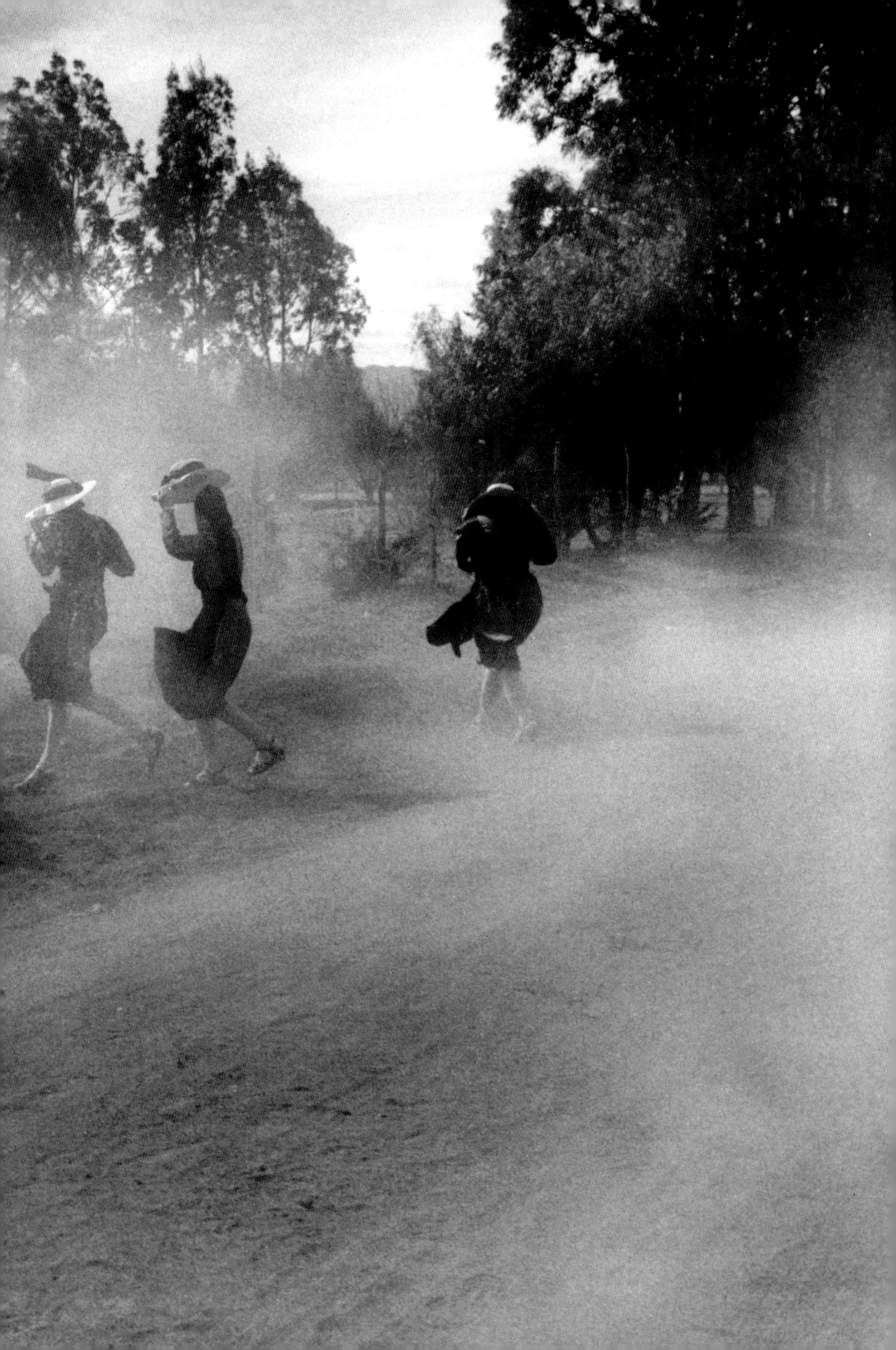

GIDEON MENDEL
Germany/
South Africa,
Network
Photographers,
UK for Tempo
Magazine,
Germany

9428

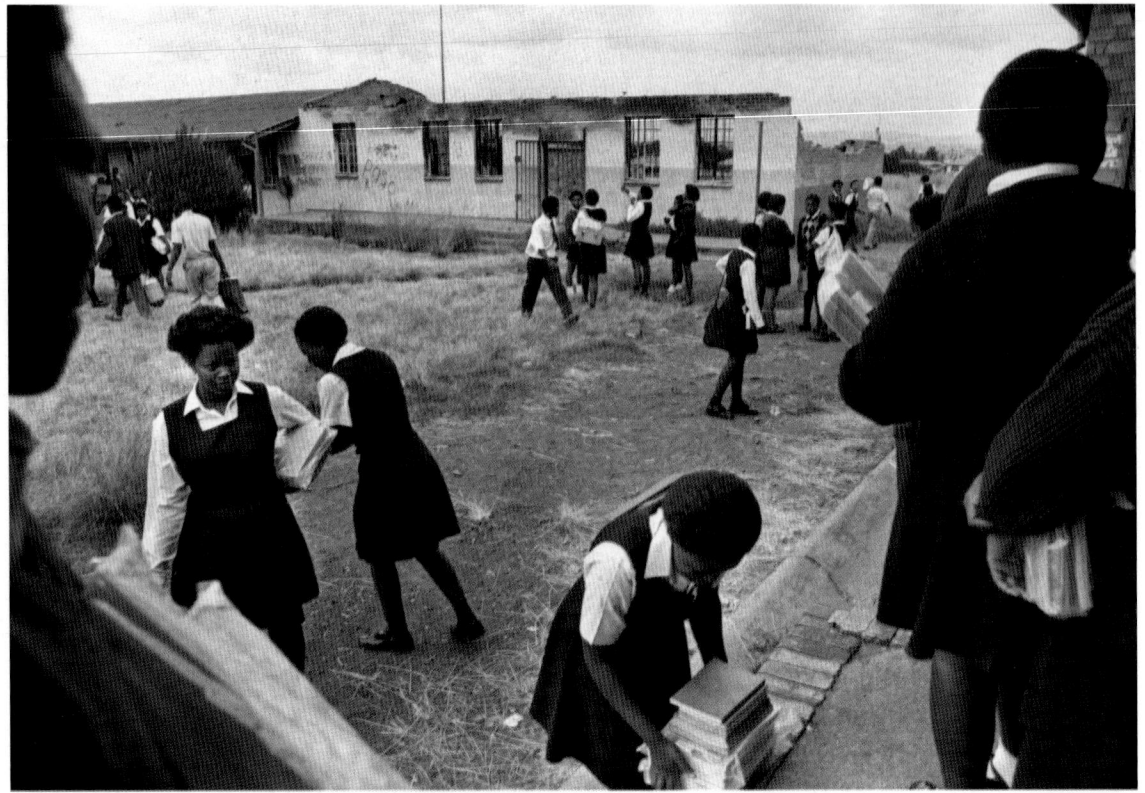

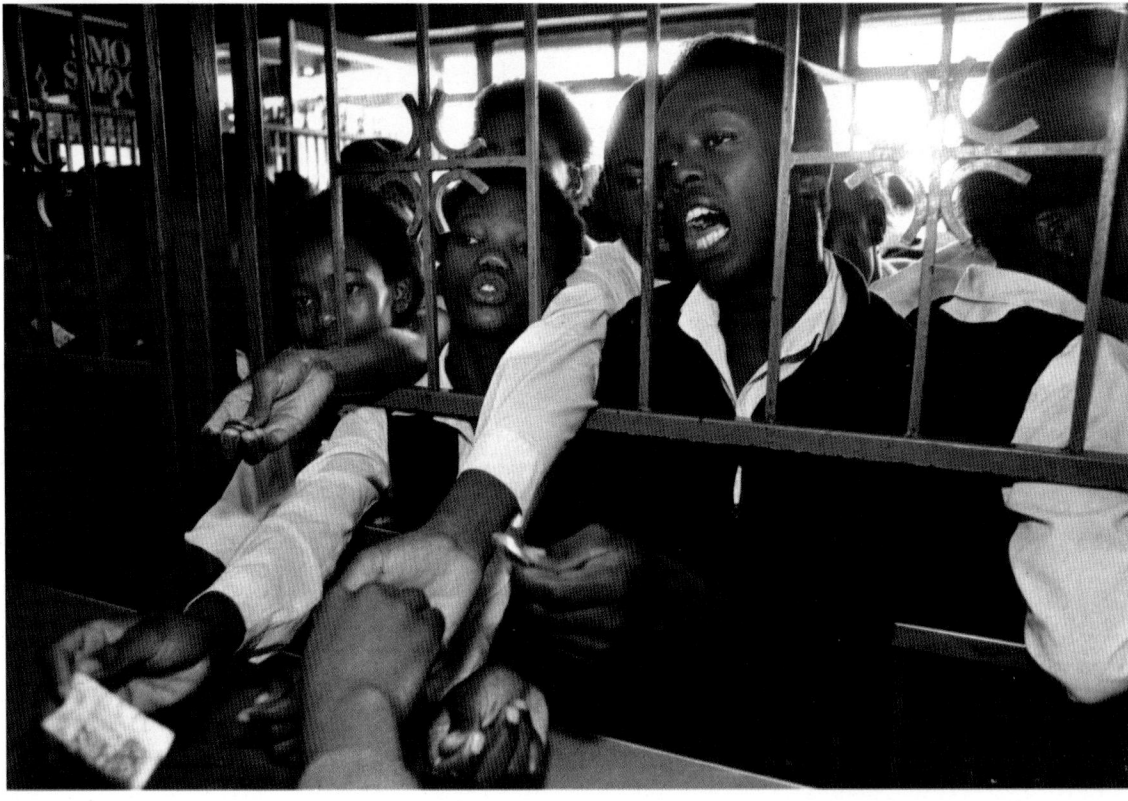

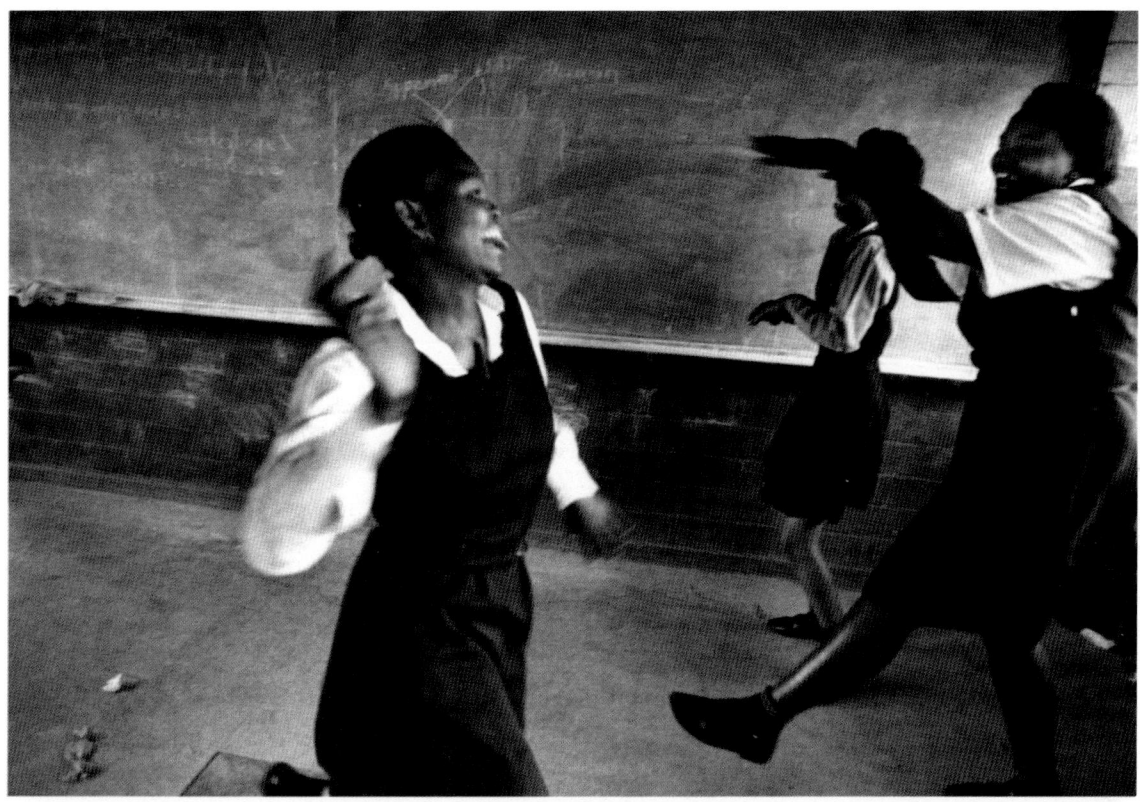

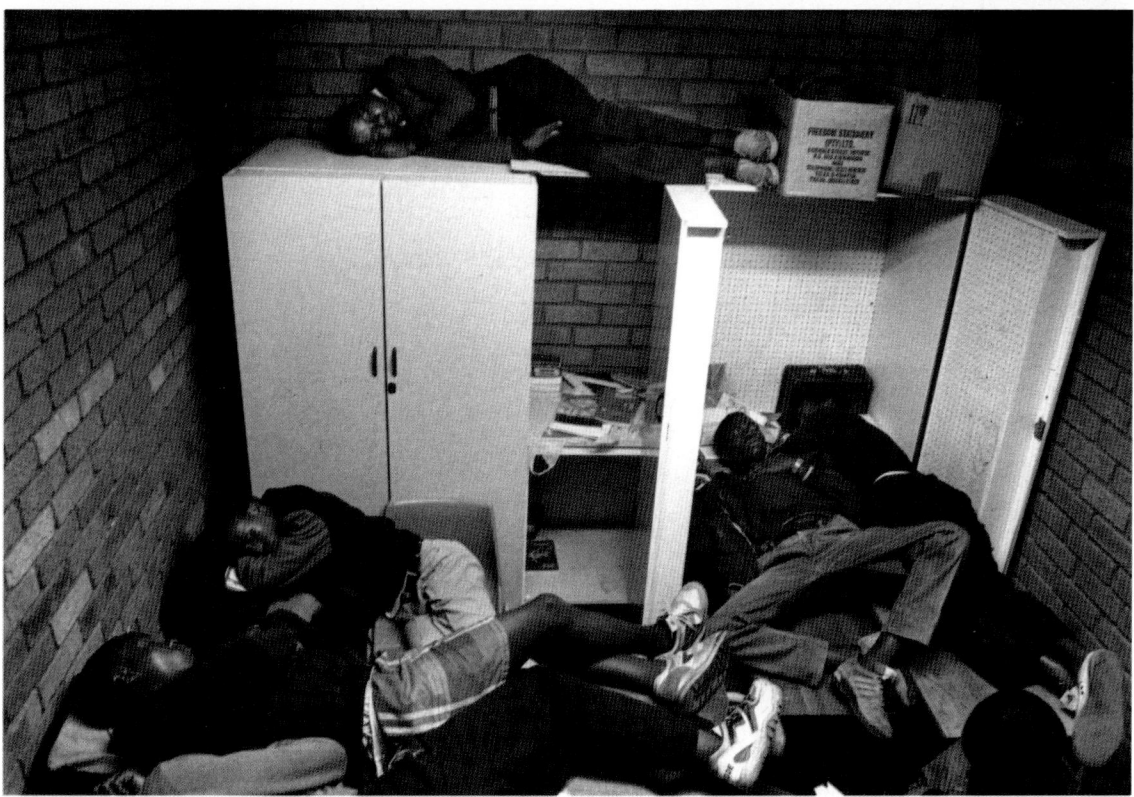

9428
The imposition of Afrikaans as the main language of instruction at Morris Isaacson School in the heart of Soweto, South Africa, was one of the things that sparked off the riots in 1976. Many of today's teachers were pupils at the time. In the wake of apartheid, educational standards are still low, but the pupils have an immense hunger for knowledge.

Facing page: Pupils head for class after morning assembly. During their lunch break, they crowd into a nearby shop to buy some food. Top: Girls perform a dance from the film *Sarafina*, which was made here. Above: After night study sessions, pupils often prefer to sleep in classrooms rather than walk through dangerous streets to overcrowded homes.

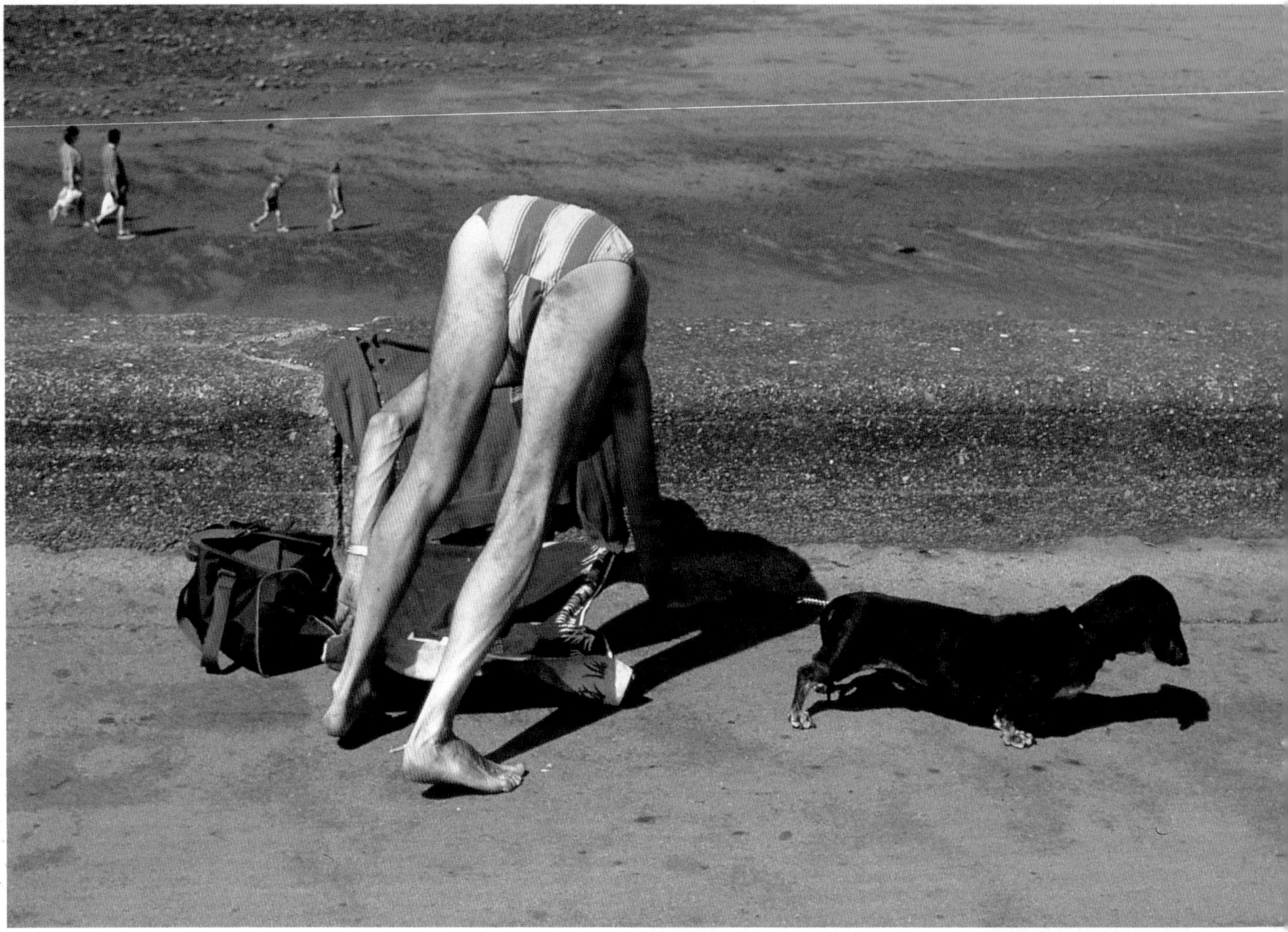

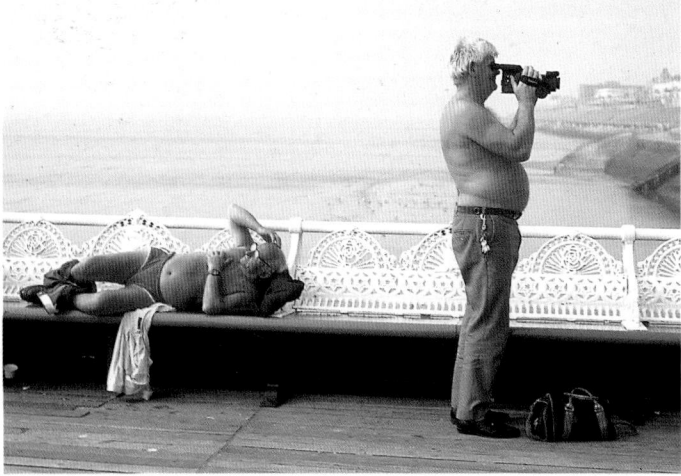
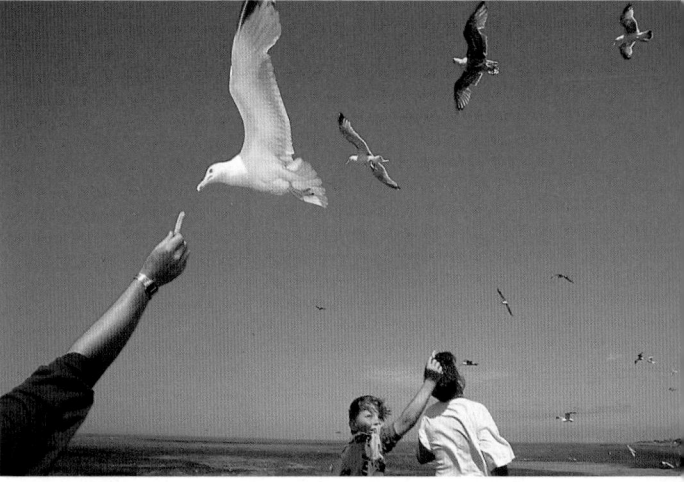

RICHARD BAKER
Katz Pictures for
Sunday Express
Magazine,
UK

**THIRD PRIZE
STORIES**

9429

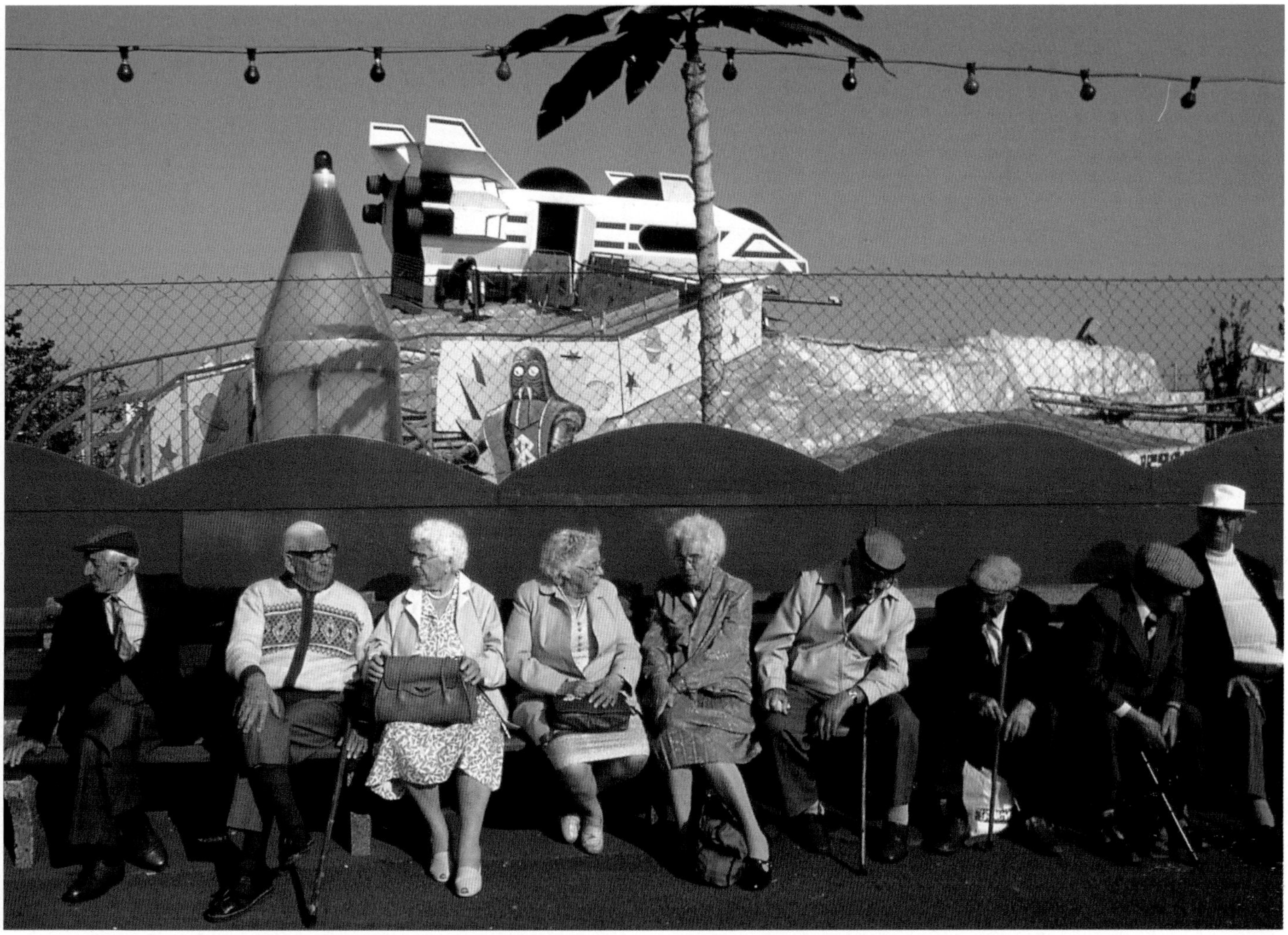

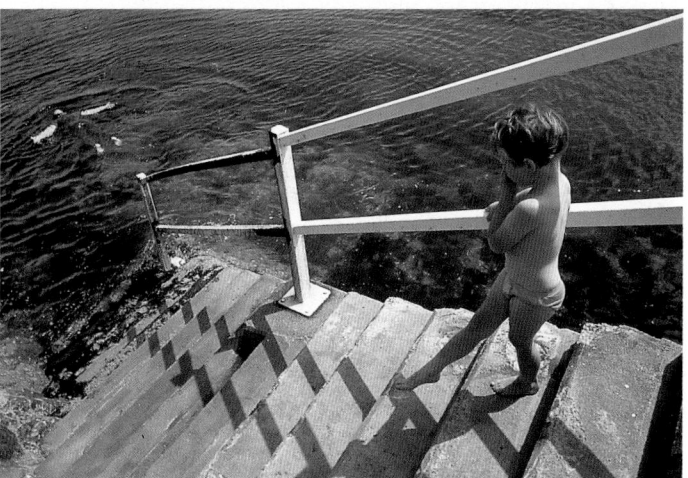

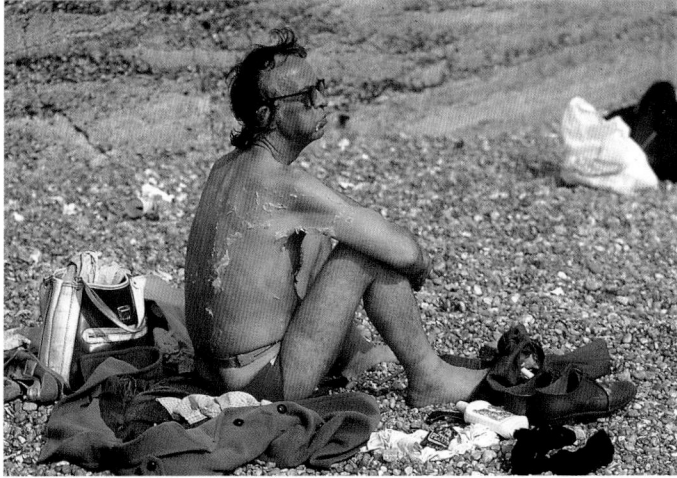

9429
Making a virtue of financial necessity, thousands of British vacationers returned to the beaches of their youth in 1993 rather than taking package trips to Mediterranean resorts. As the economic recession forced them to tighten their belts, they rediscovered their own country's beaches for a cheap and cheerful holiday.

The photographer observed them letting their hair down in resorts all over England, on sandy and pebble beaches, on piers and promenades. He pictured them in Great Yarmouth (facing page, top), Dover (facing page, bottom right), Minehead (top and above), Blackpool (above left) and Paignton (far left).

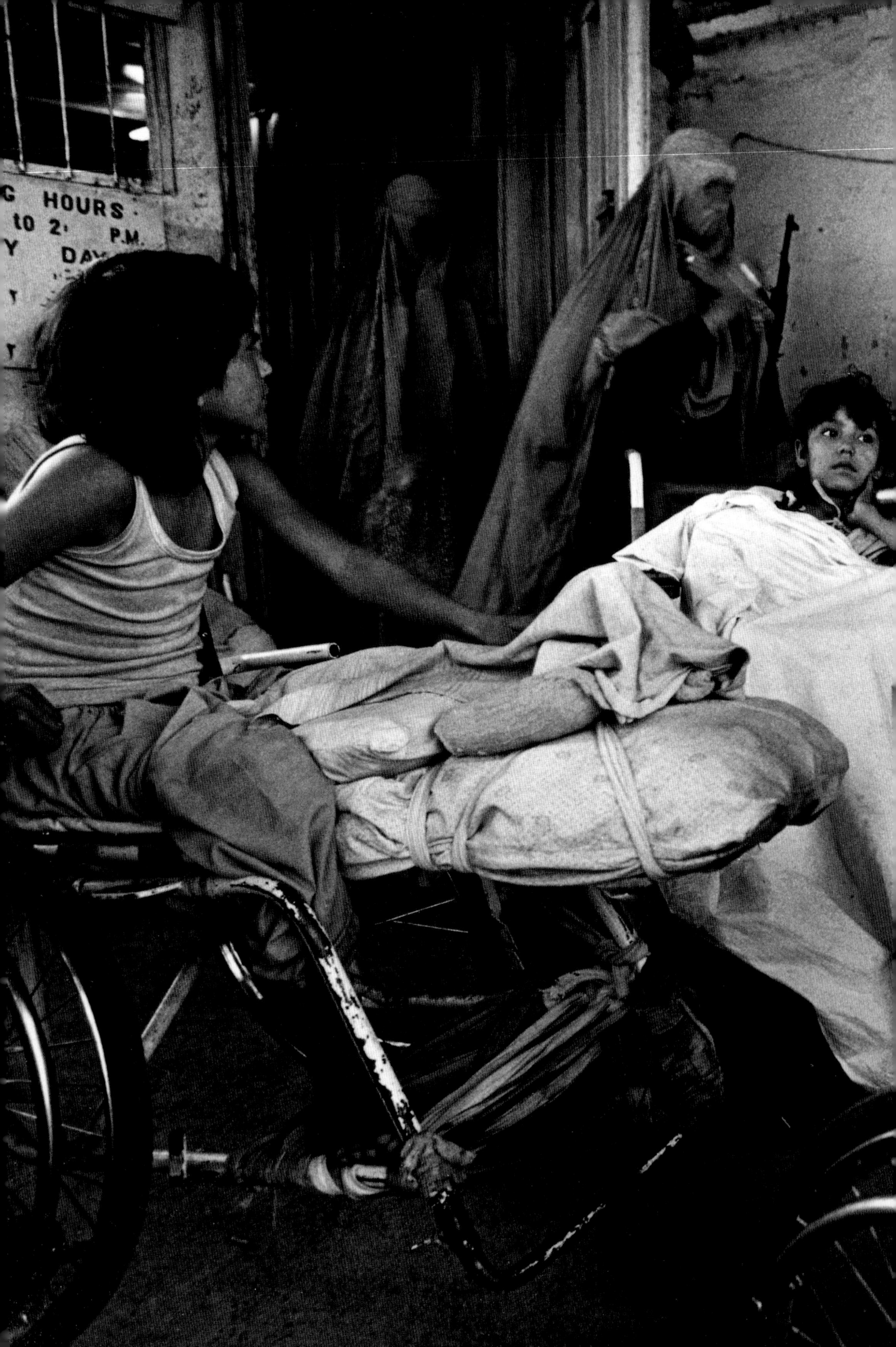

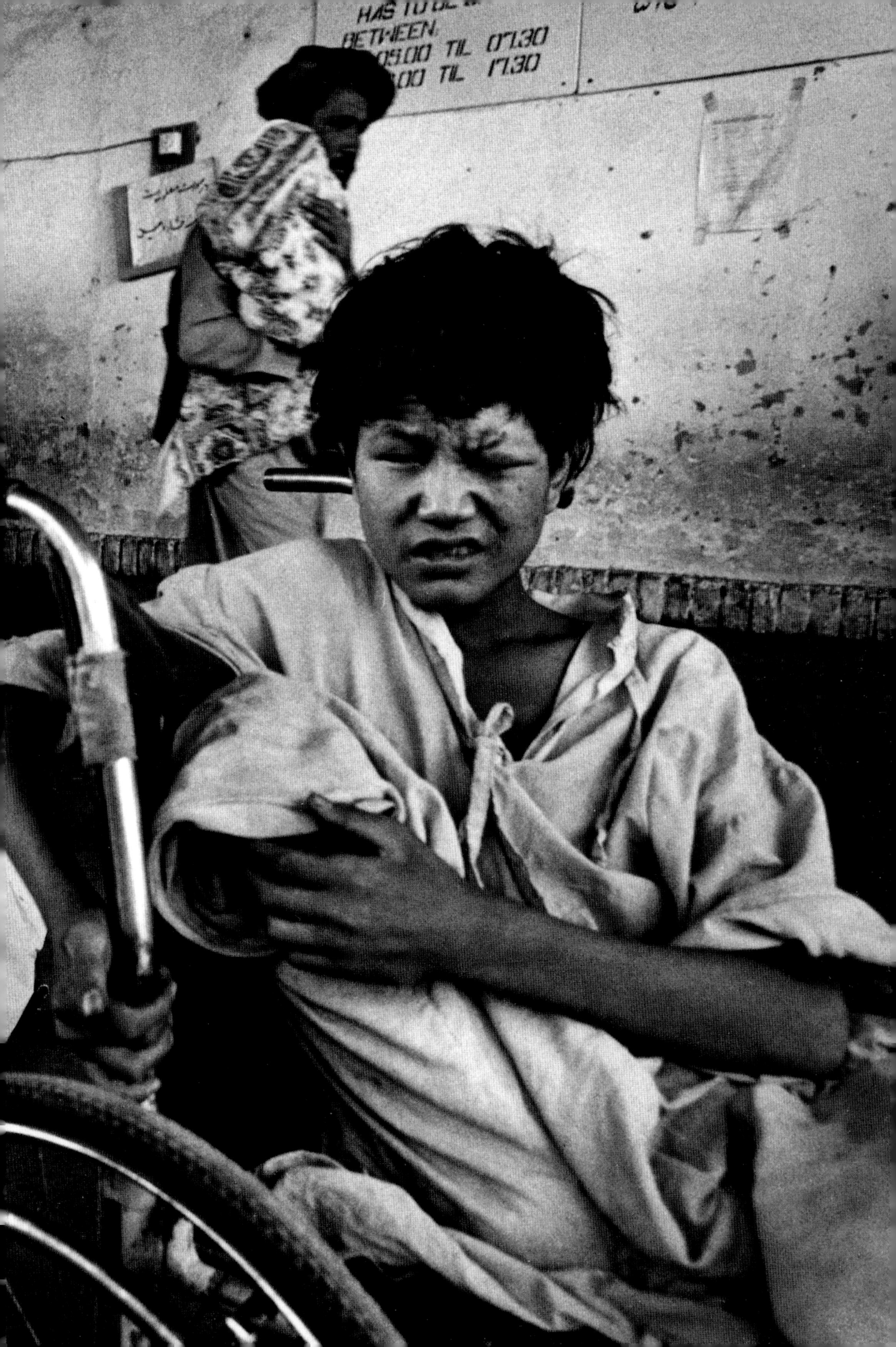

JOHN REARDON
Katz Pictures for
Observer
Magazine,
UK

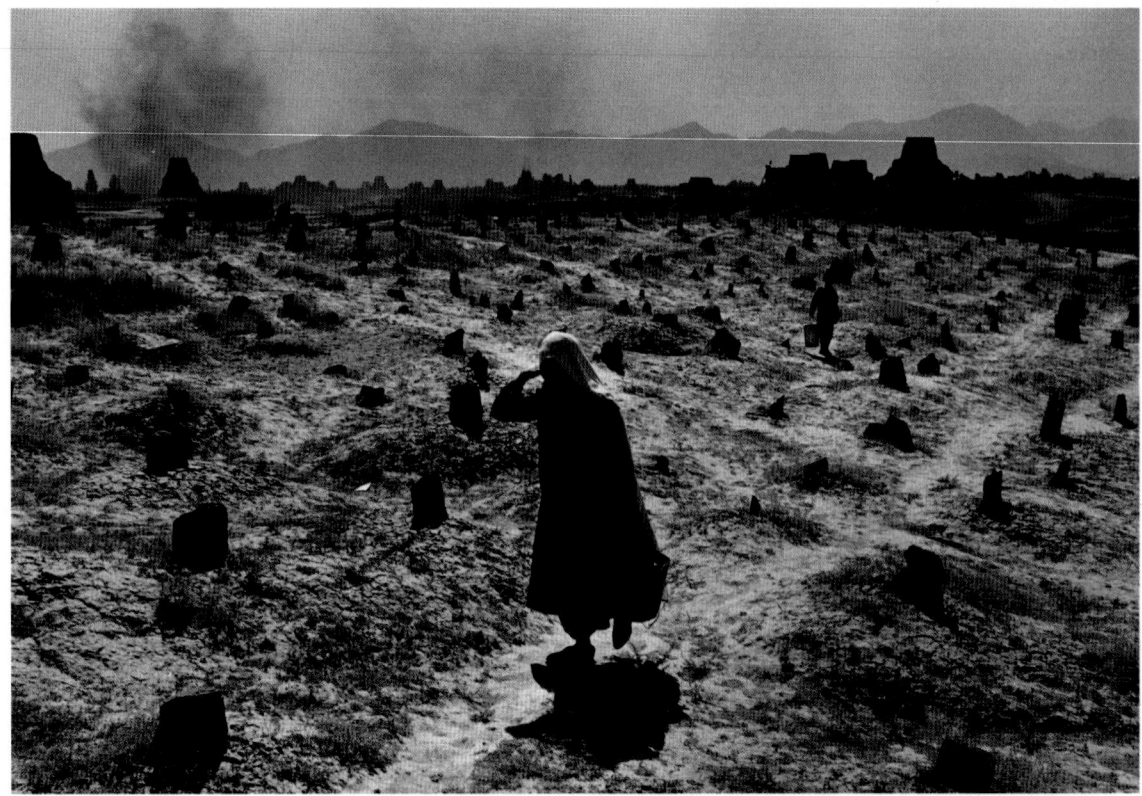

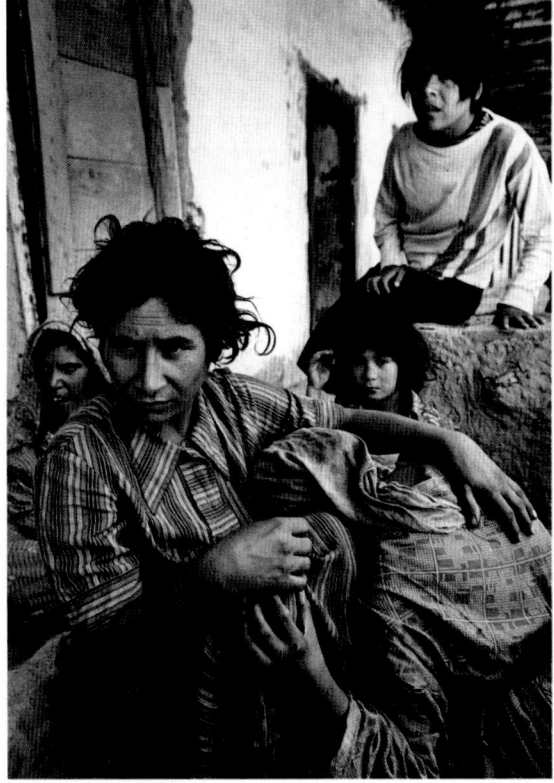

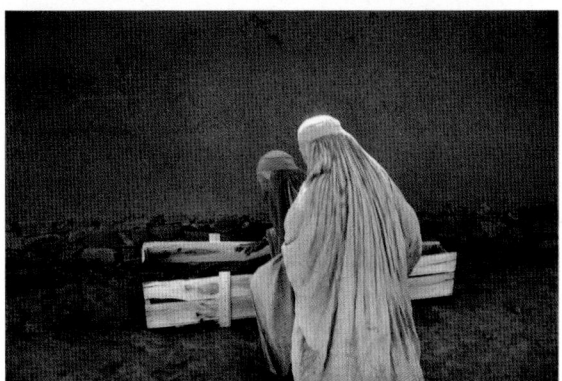

9430 (story starts on p.70)
Although the war is officially over, fighting continues in Afghanistan. While the world turned its attention to what was happening elsewhere, thousands were killed in the streets of Kabul. Previous pages: Victims of the civil war at Karte-Se Hospital in the Afghan capital.

Top and above right: Coffins and cemeteries are daily realities in the lives of Kabul's women. Above: The nursing staff abandoned this mental hospital, leaving the 160 patients to fend for themselves. Facing page: A bus stops at a mujahedin checkpoint. A 12-year-old boy weeps for his father, killed in the streets patrolled by General Dostom's men.

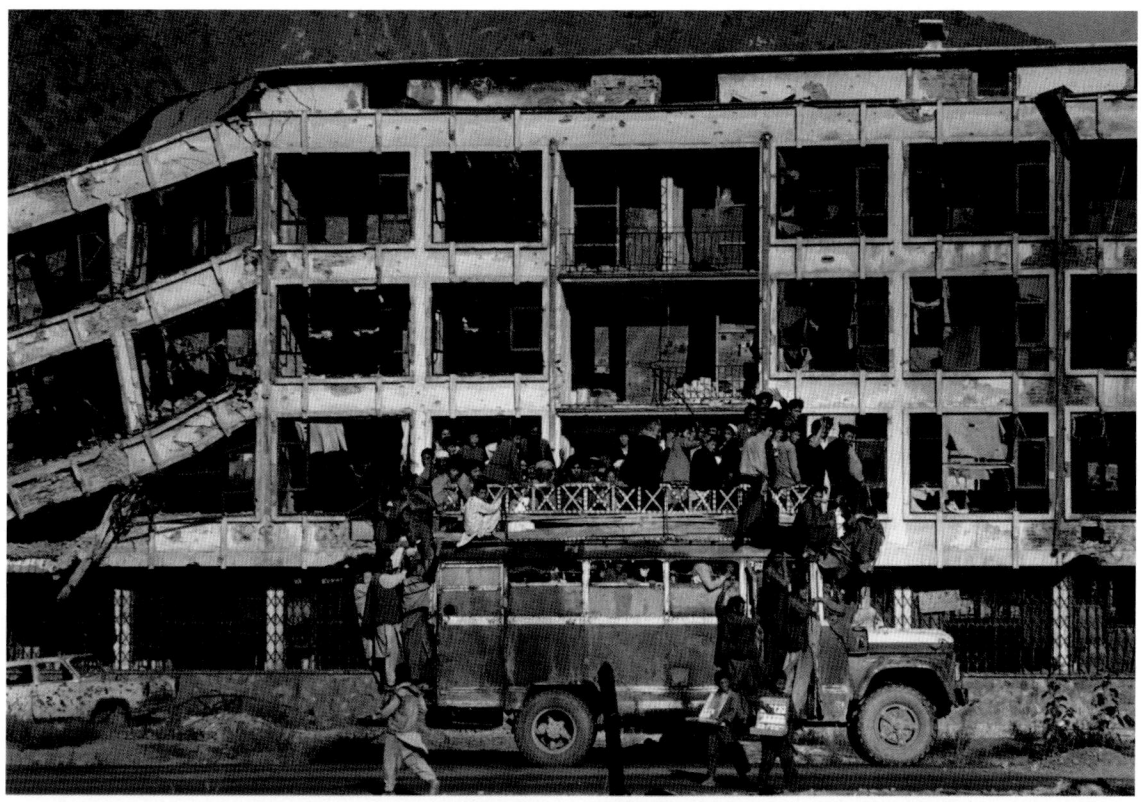

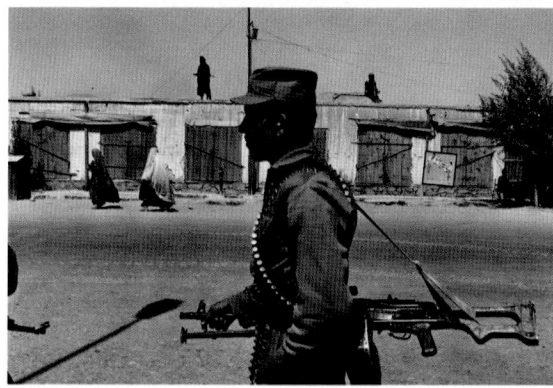

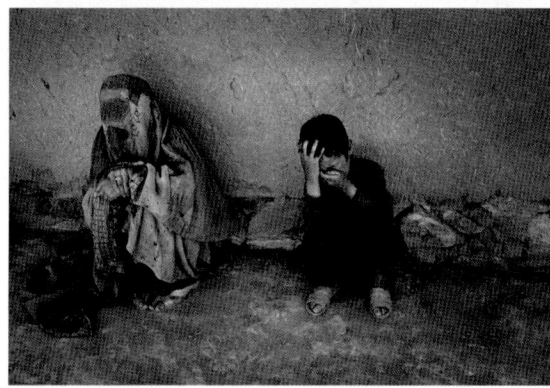

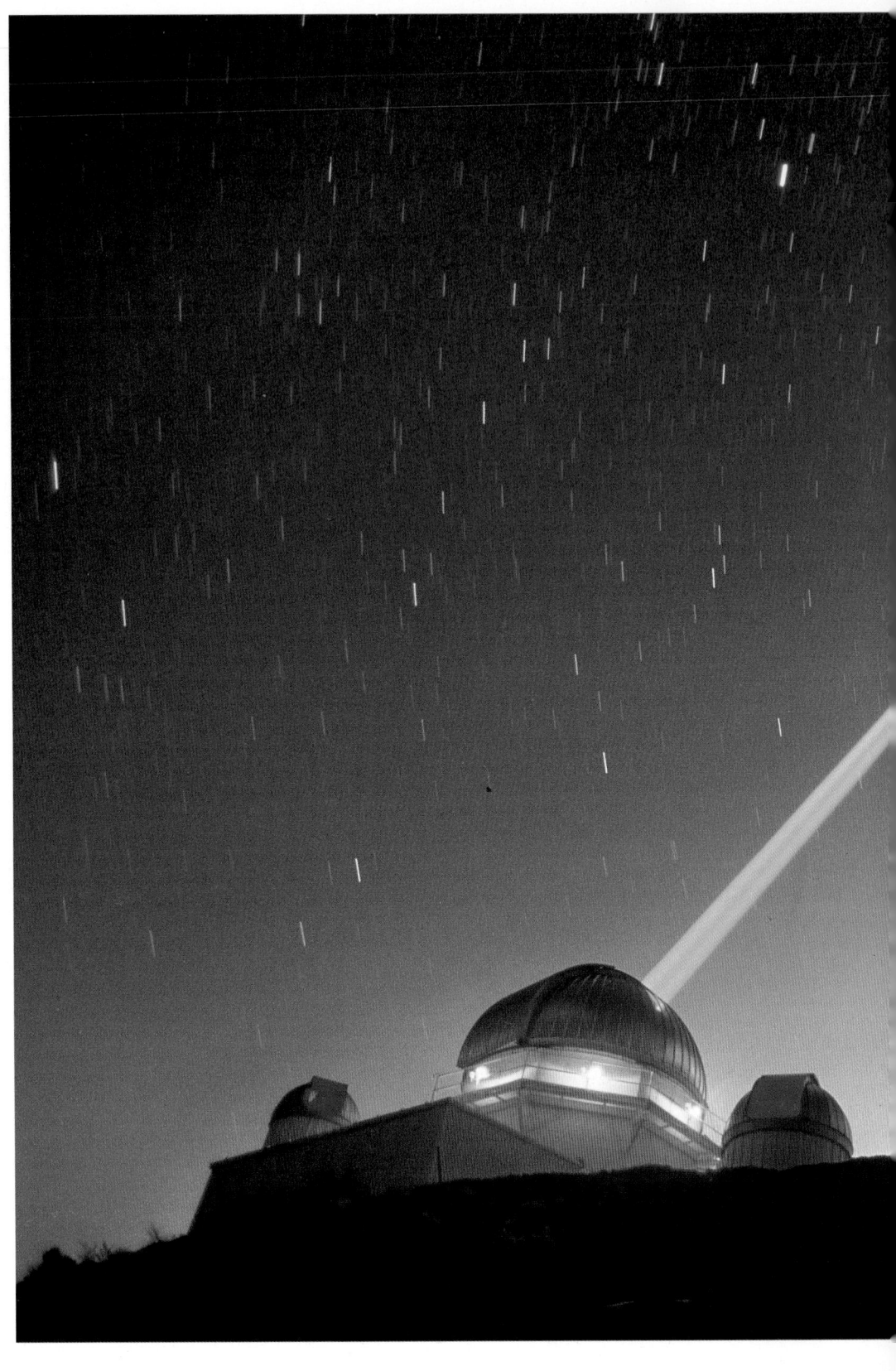

SCIENCE AND TECHNOLOGY

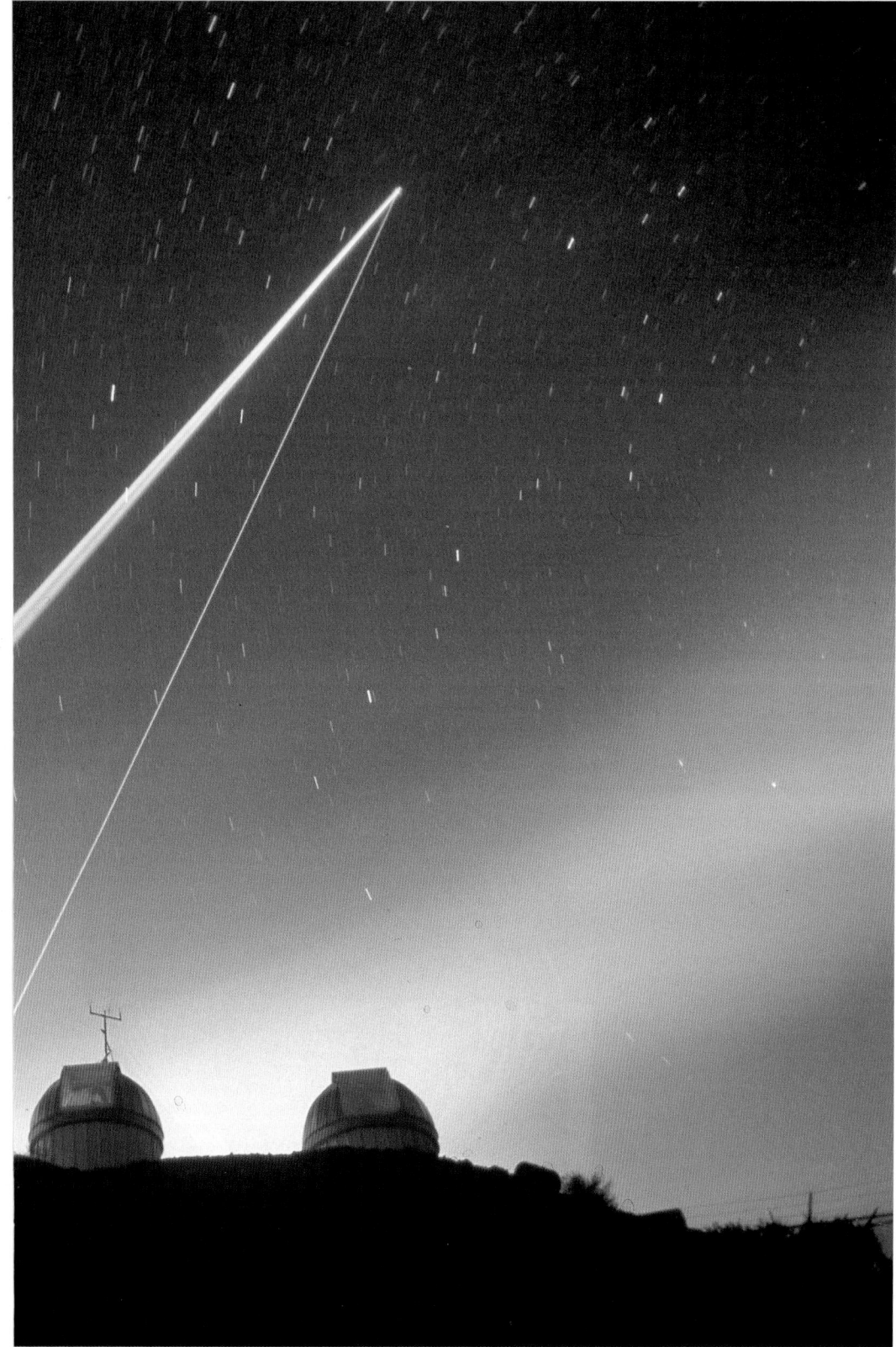

ROGER H. RESSMEYER
Ressmeyer-Starlight
for National
Geographic Magazine,
USA

**FIRST PRIZE
SINGLES** (left)

**FIRST PRIZE
STORIES**

9431

9431
Leading edge technology enables scientists to examine even the most remote reaches of the universe. All over the world they are probing and measuring, trying to understand what until now no one has understood. Distorting atmospheric effects are studied laser beams, and computers use telescope optics to create images of unprecedented clarity.

At the Starfire Optical Range in New Mexico (above), a green copper-vapor laser and an orange sodium-wavelength laser are aimed through telescopes. Gases in specific layers of the atmosphere reflect the laser light, creating artificial stars (story continues).

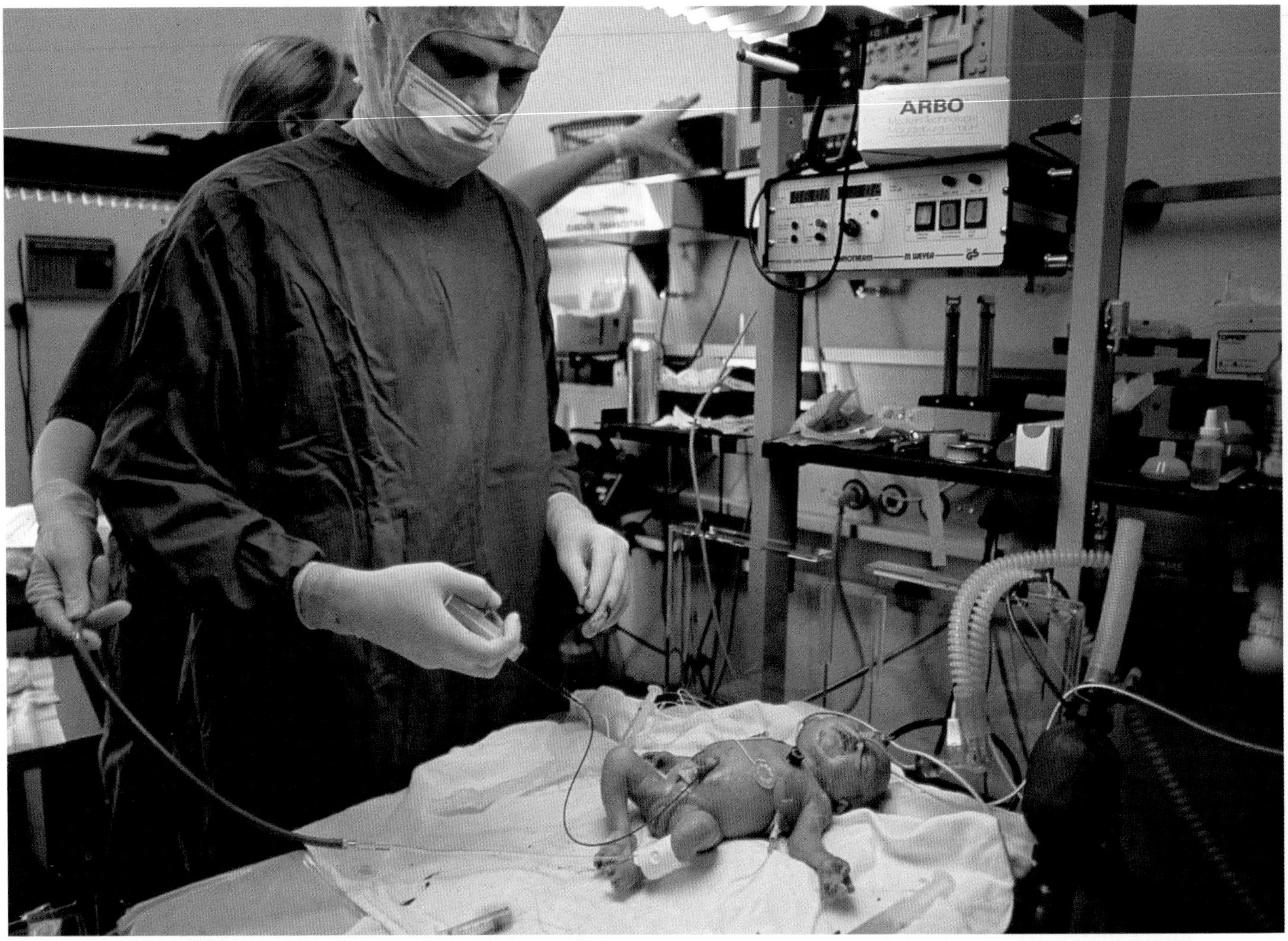

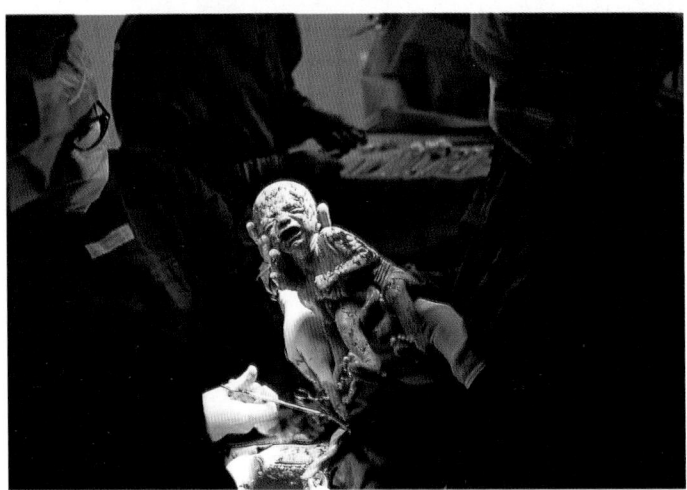
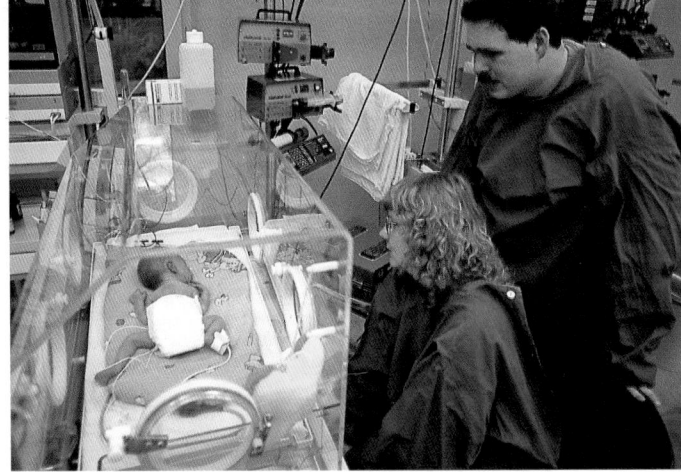

**RONALD
FROMMANN**
Stern Magazine,
Germany

**SECOND PRIZE
SINGLES**
(facing page, top)

**THIRD PRIZE
STORIES**

9432

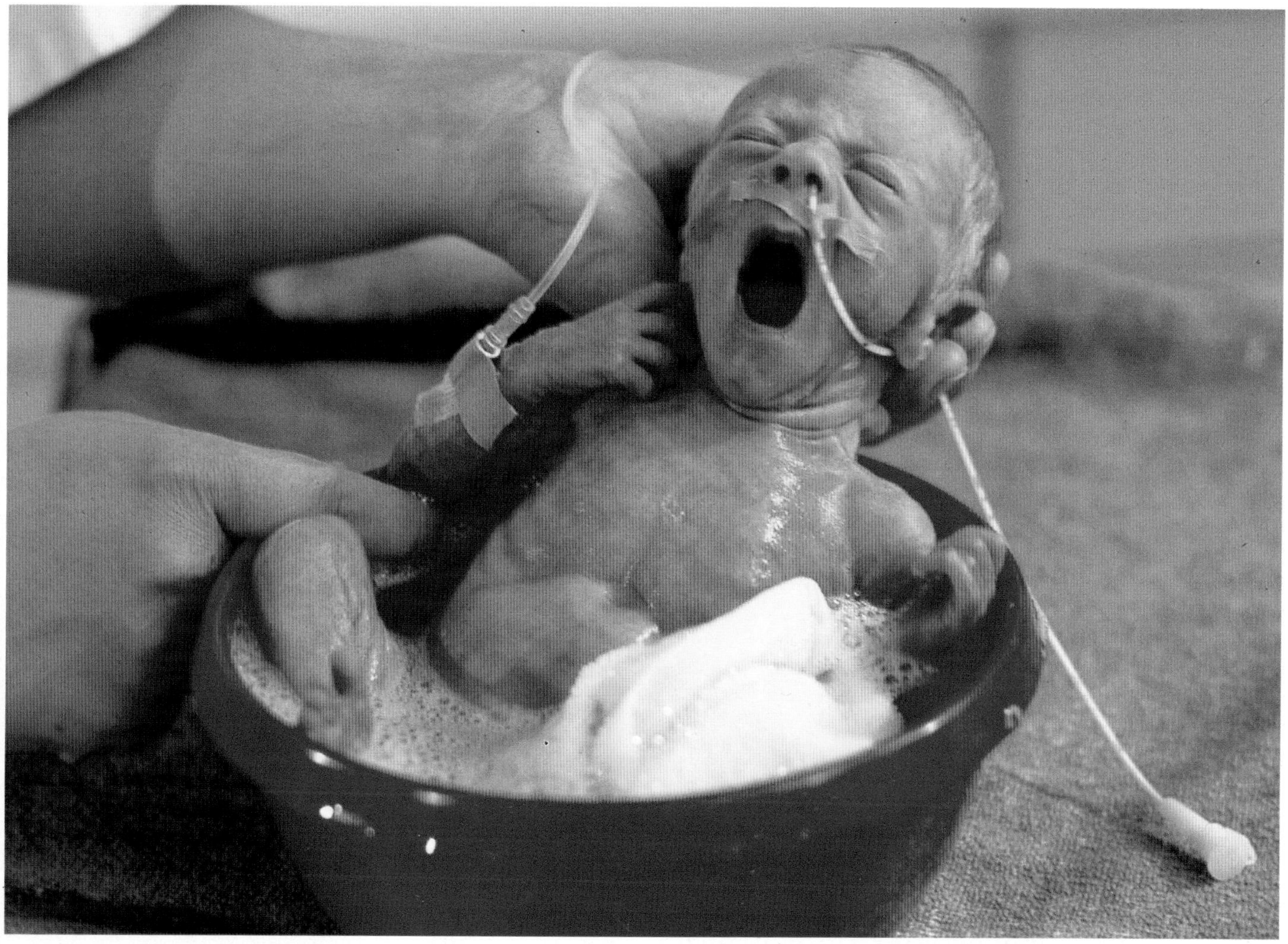

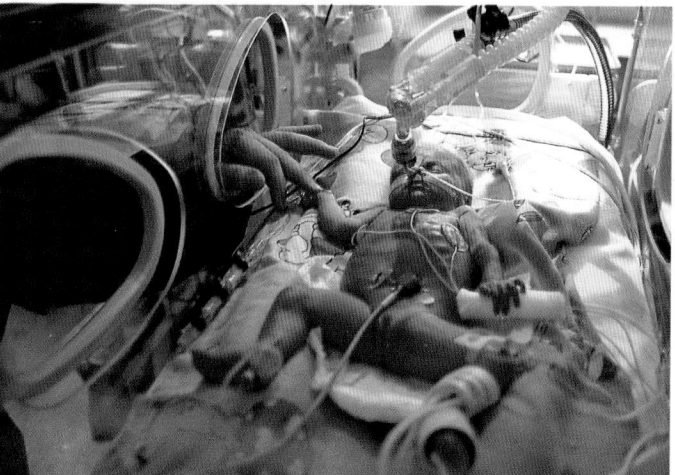

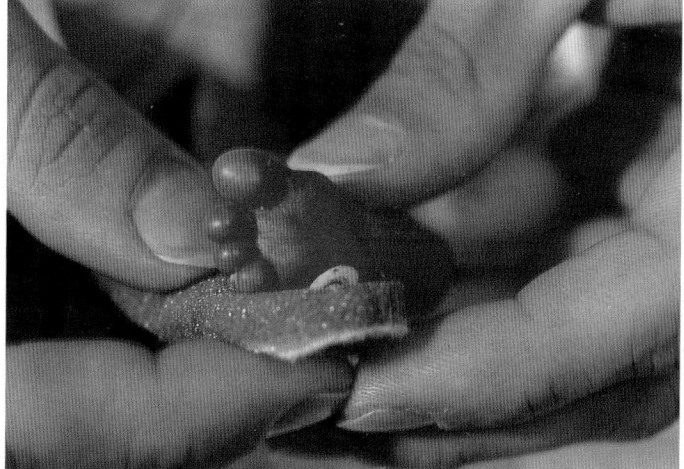

9432
This neonatal center in Dortmund, Germany, specializes in high-risk and premature births. Infants born three months early, some weighing as little as 500 grams, are no exception here. They are kept alive with the latest techniques and around-the-clock nursing care, but even so, most babies born before the 26th week of pregnancy suffer permanent damage.

Facing page: Premature babies shortly after they were born. A catheter is attached to the foot of an infant to establish the oxygen level in the blood. This page, top: At three weeks old, this child weighs just 1200 grams. A salad bowl serves as its bath. Parents can do little but watch helplessly as their role is filled by doctors and nurses.

GILLES SAUSSIER
Gamma, France,
for Life Magazine,
USA

**THIRD PRIZE
SINGLES**
(facing page, top)

9433

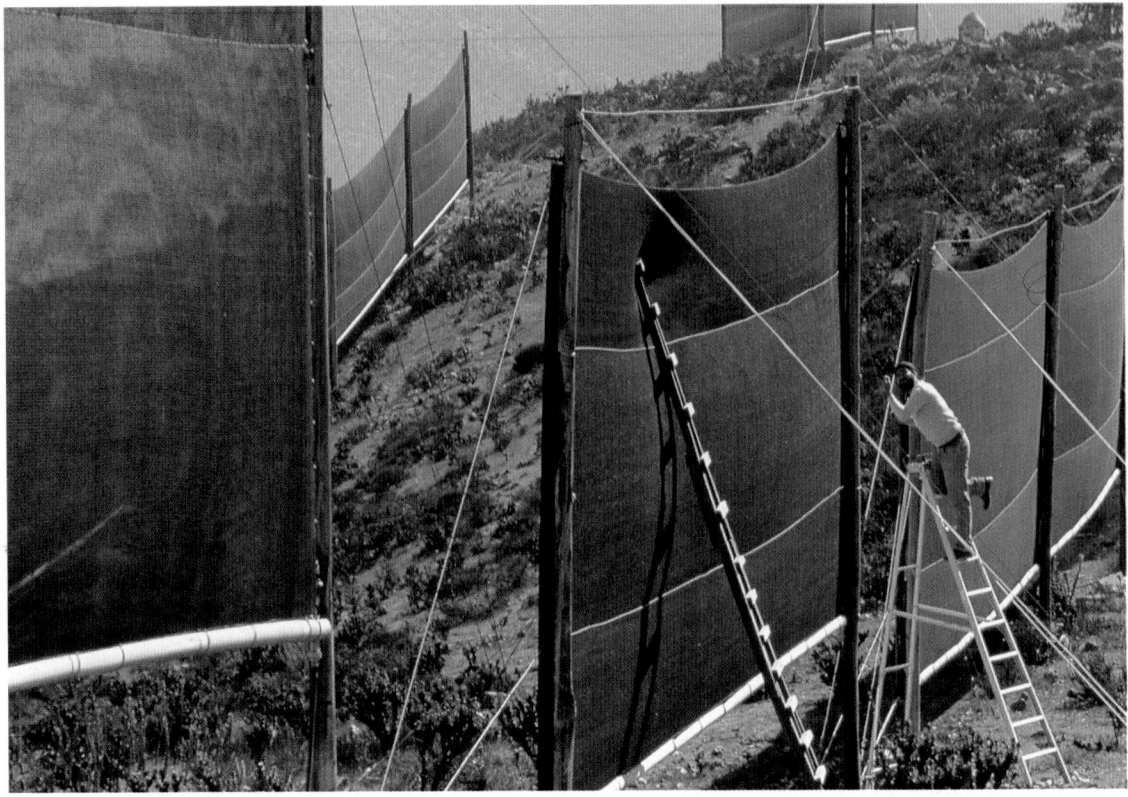

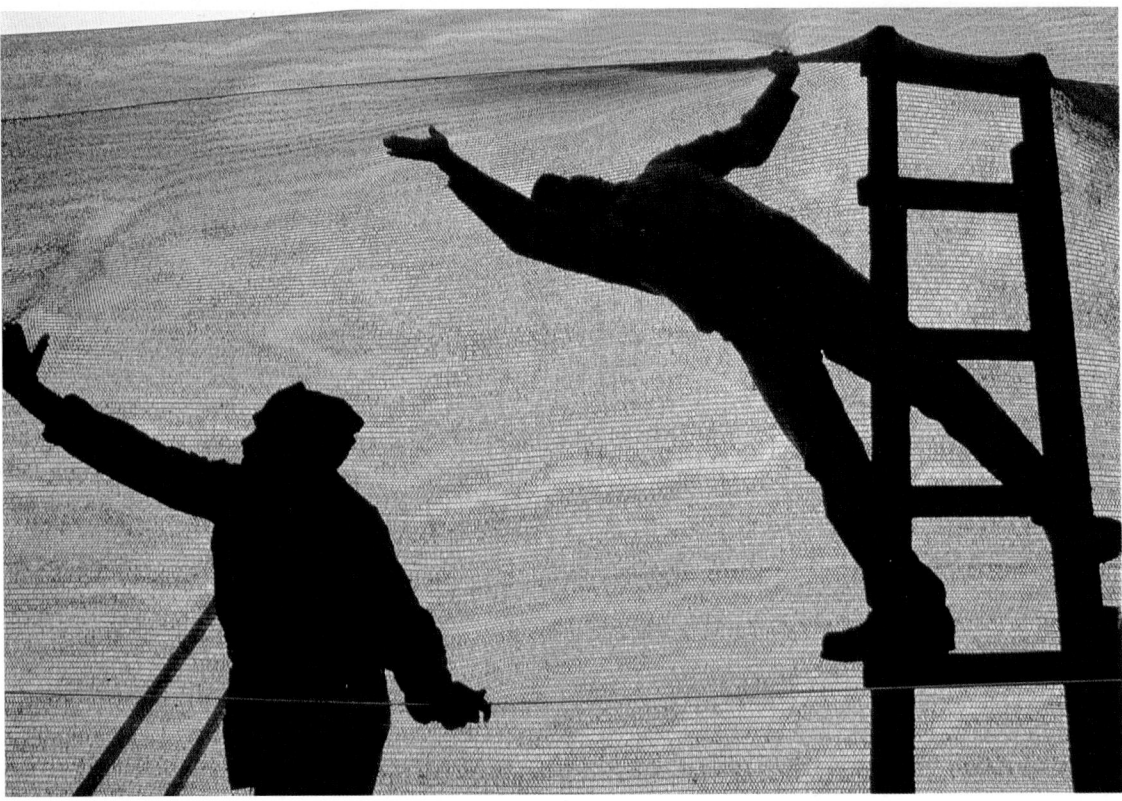

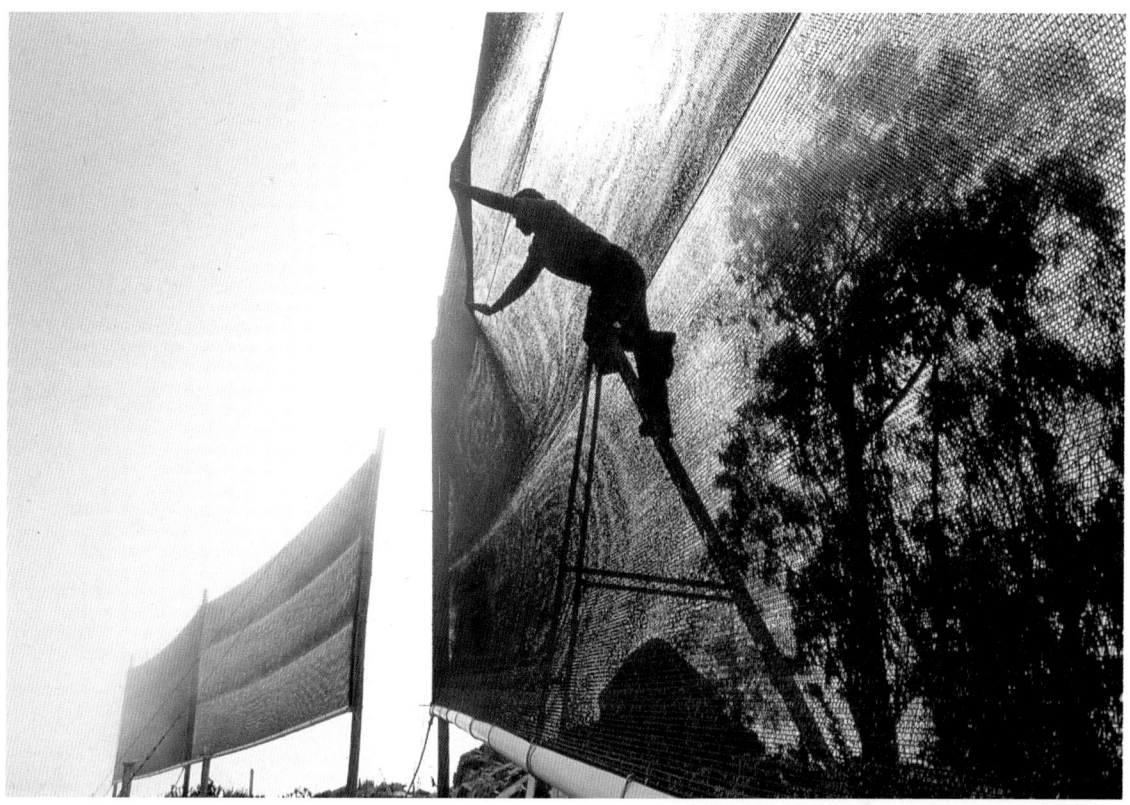

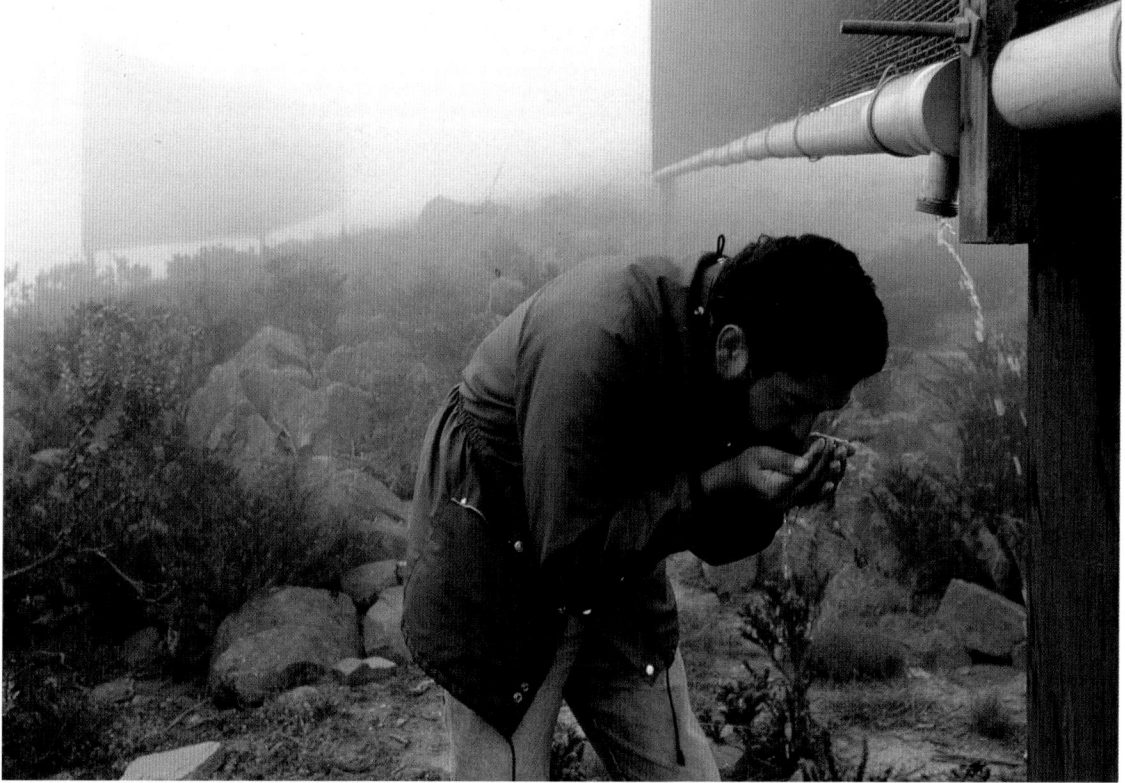

9433

Drinking the sky: an unorthodox water collection project funded jointly by the Chilean and Canadian governments. The Andean foothills on Chile's northern coast are enveloped in an almost permanent ribbon of clouds, which rarely produce rain. An ingenious system has now been developed to catch droplets of fog in giant nylon nets, suspended between wooden posts.

The water trapped in the fine mesh netting trickles down into a trough and is filtered and piped to a 96,000-liter storage tank. The system needs only two men to maintain it. This cheap, low-tech way of harvesting water for the nearby village of Chungungo has excited interest in more than 20 countries with similar climatic conditions.

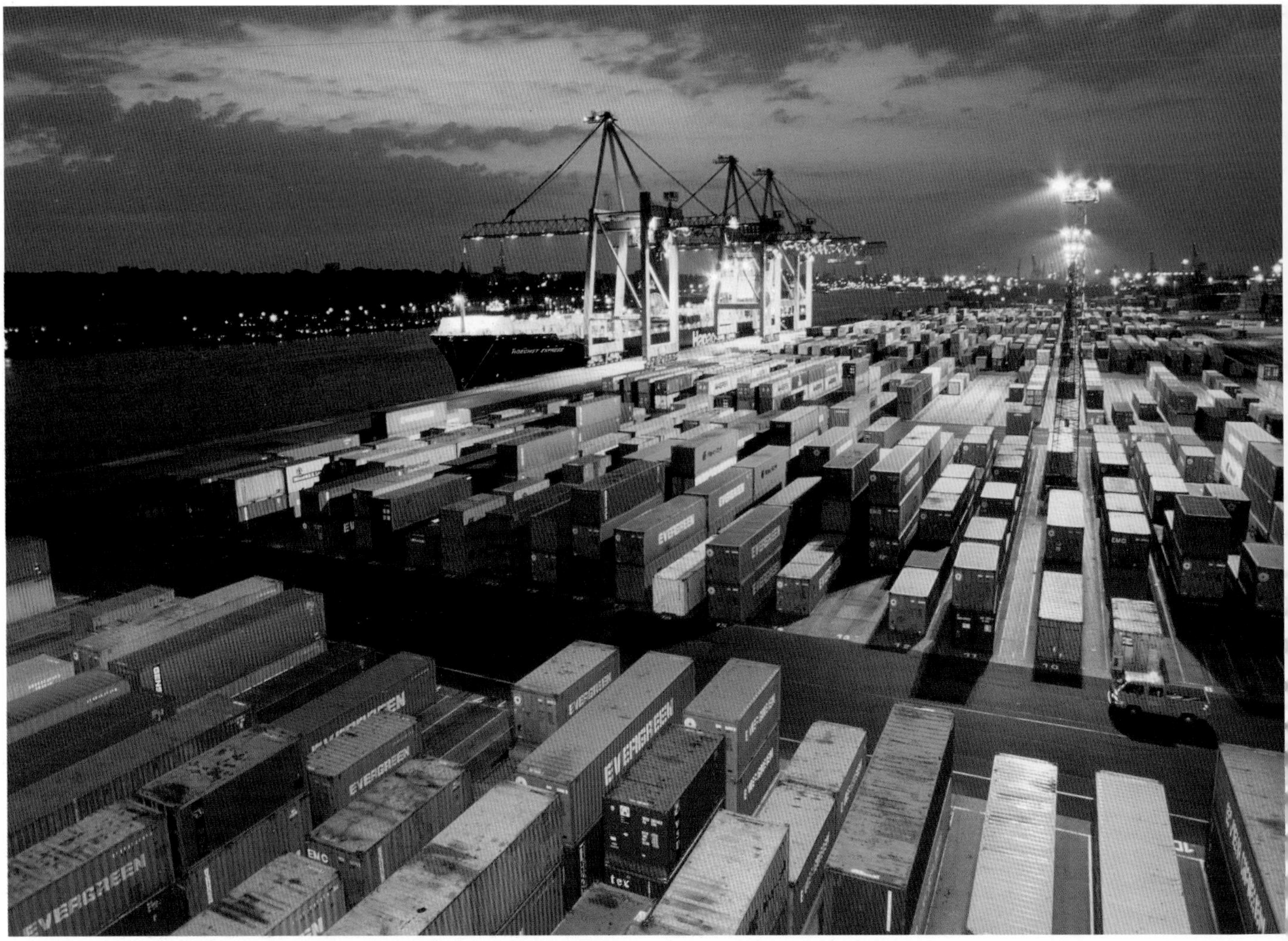

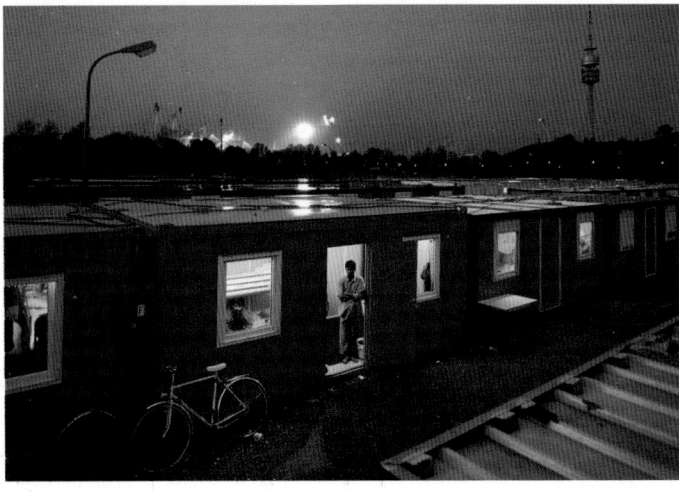
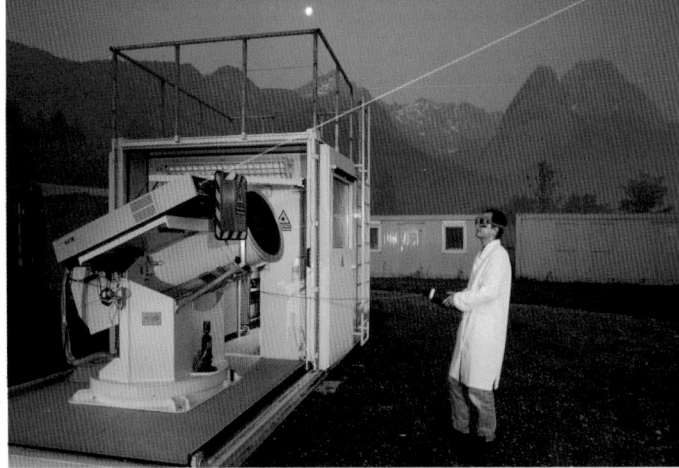

DIRK EISERMANN
Das Fotoarchiv for
Stern Magazine,
Germany

**SECOND PRIZE
STORIES**

9434

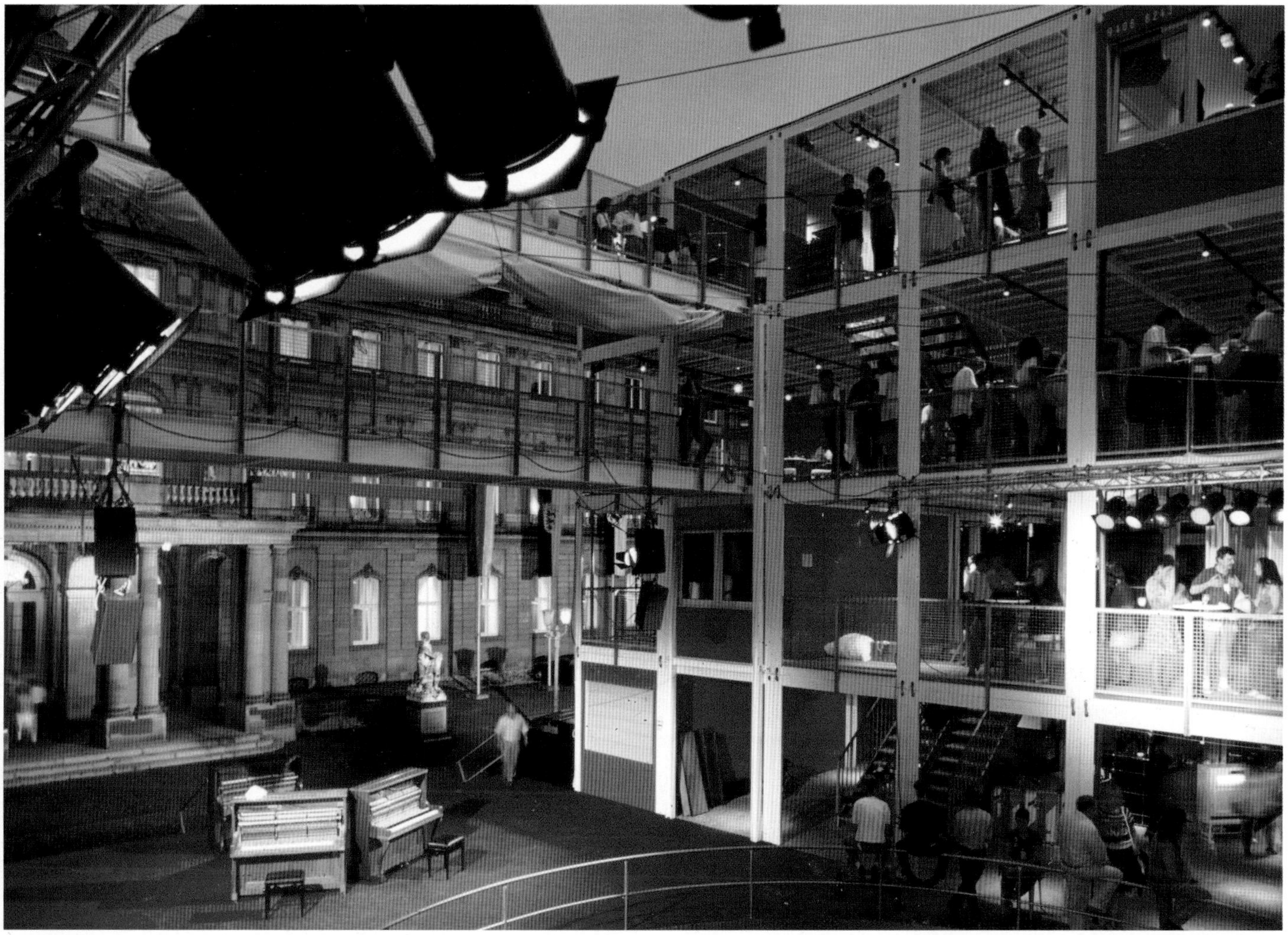

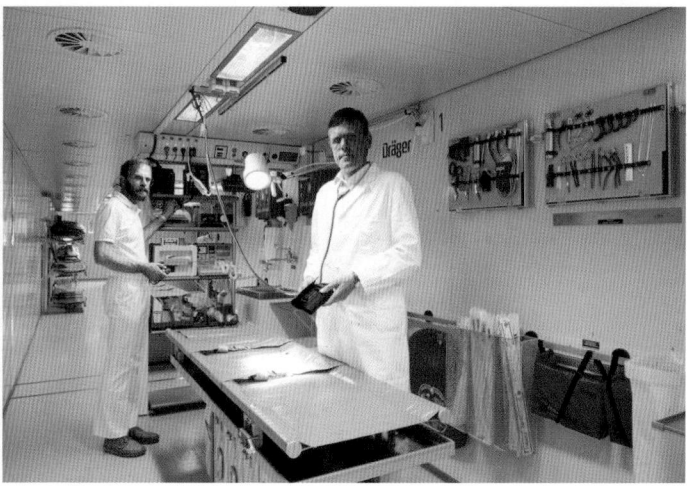

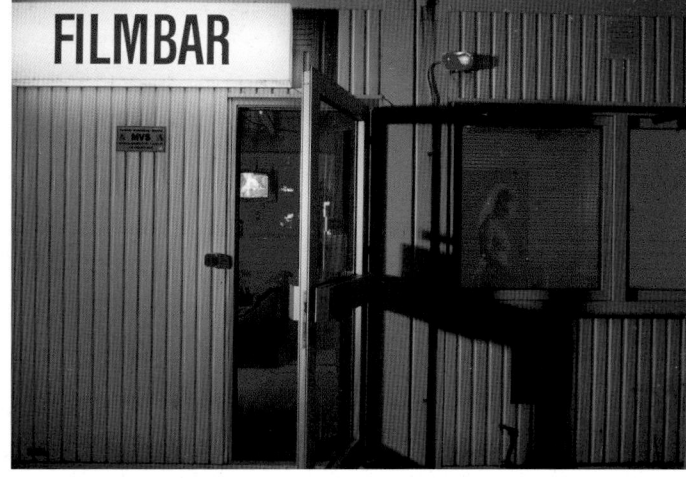

9434
Boxes of tricks: the versatility of the metal container. Originally designed to transport goods – Hamburg's Burchard Quay (facing page, top) has space for 12,000 – containers have proved amazingly adaptable. In Munich they are inhabited by Sri Lankan refugees, and the prestigious Fraunhofer Institute uses a container for laser research of the atmosphere (bottom).

This page, top: At the 1993 World Athletics Championships in Stuttgart, the VIP center was composed of 150 linked containers. Containers are also used to save lives and satisfy lust: the pictures above show a mobile operating theater for train crashes in tunnels, and a sex cinema-cum-brothel near Berlin.

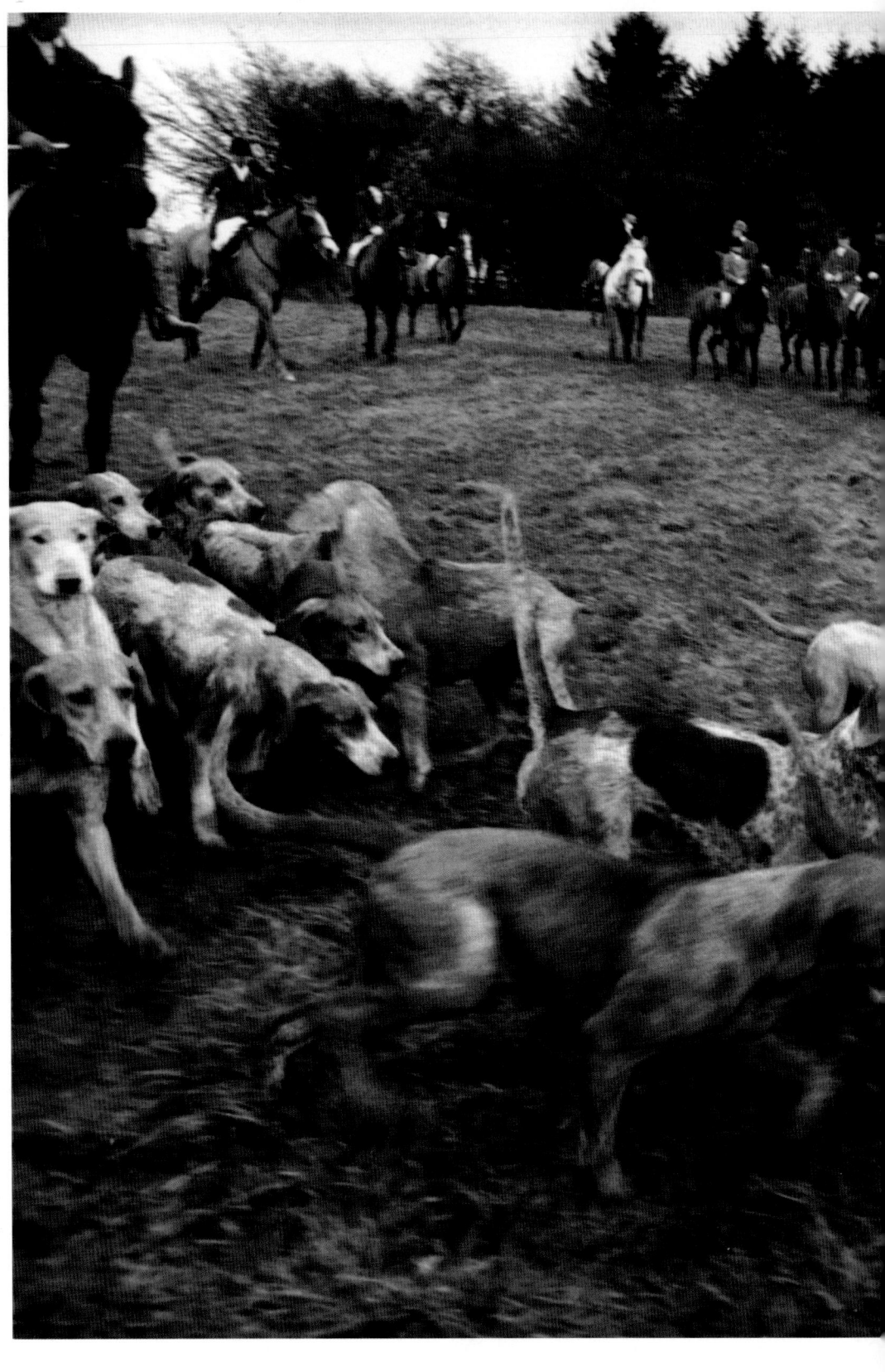

NATURE AND THE ENVIRONMENT

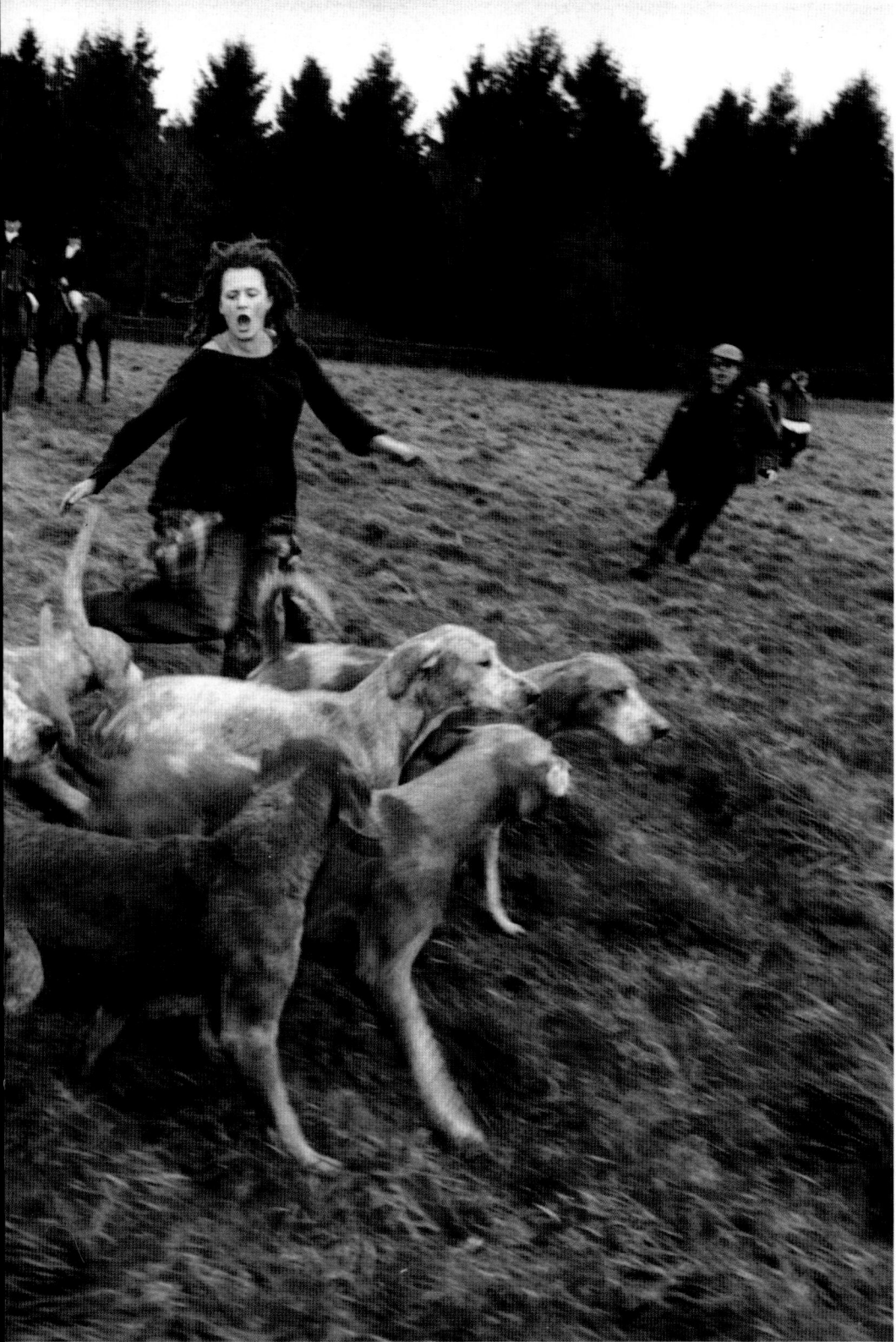

ANDREW TESTA
Reportage Magazine,
UK

**THIRD PRIZE
SINGLES**

9435

9435
Sabotage campaigns have been a feature of
the English fox-hunting season for many
years. Every season has its incidents and
accidents, and recently hunts have begun hir-
ing security firms to confront the saboteurs.
Above, a woman tries to disrupt the Surrey
Union hunt by splitting the pack of hounds.

CLAUDIO HERDENER
Editorial Atlántida,
Argentina

**FIRST PRIZE
SINGLES**

9436

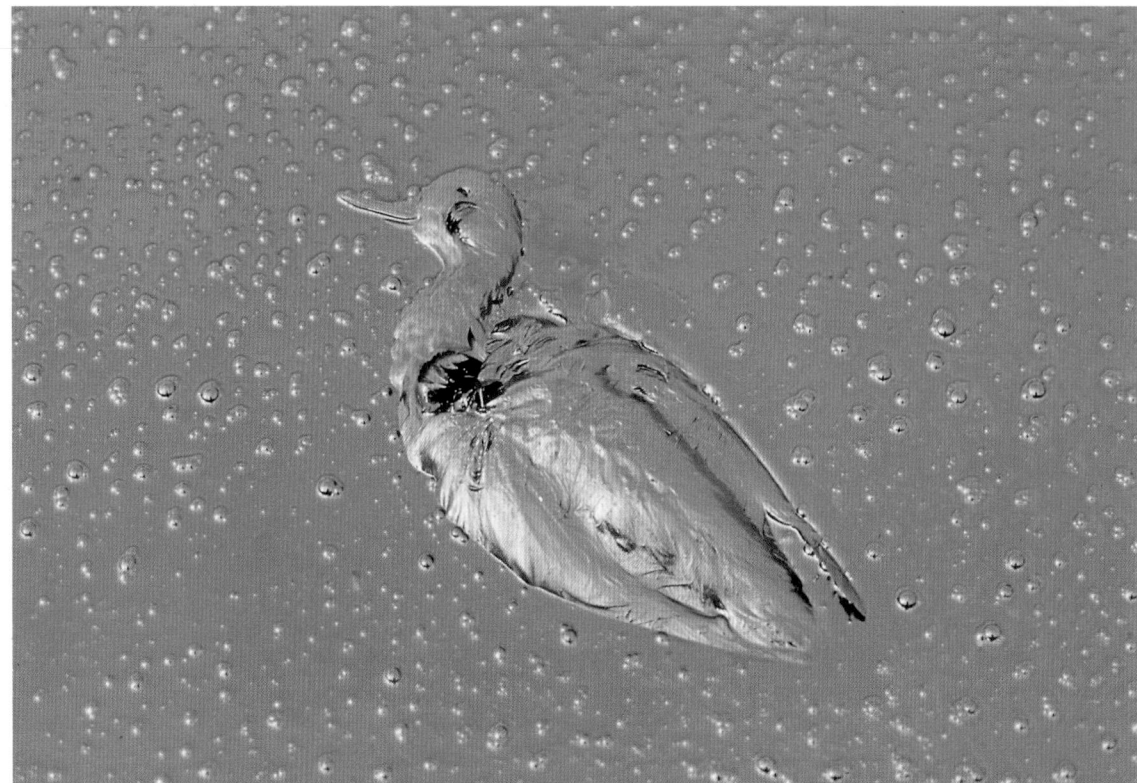

JACK PICONE
Australia,
Network
Photographers,
UK

9437

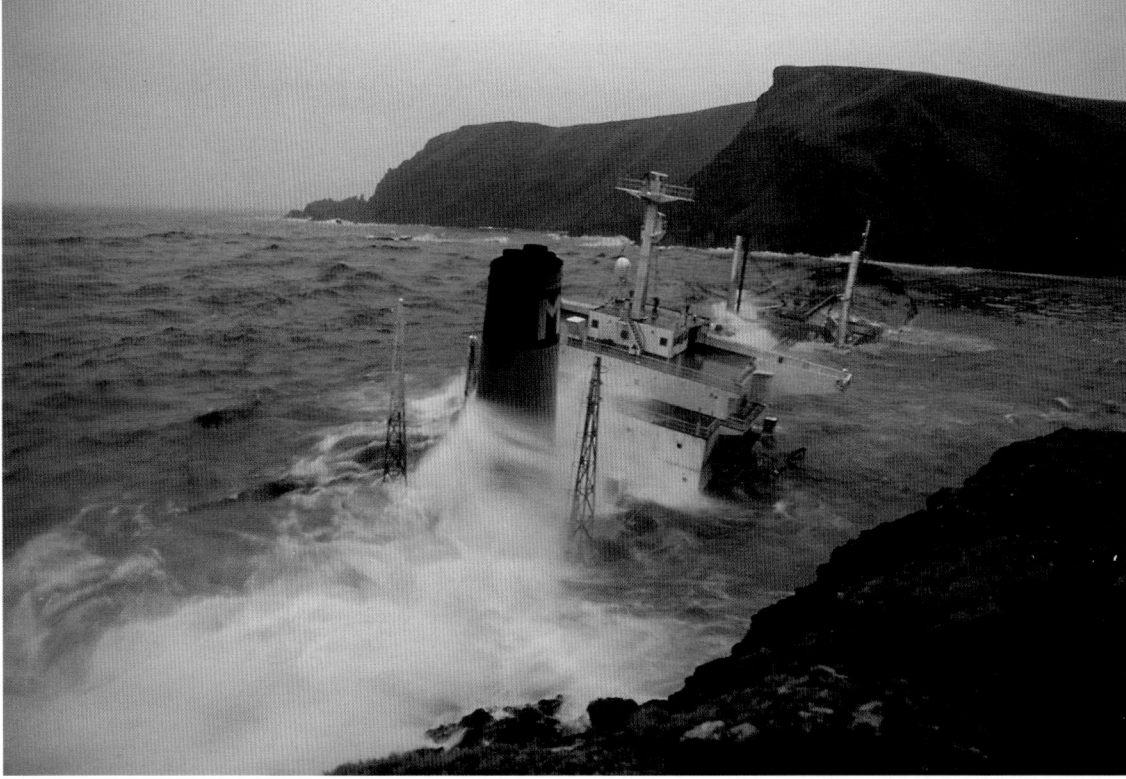

9436
In Patagonia, Argentina, some 80,000 birds die every year after getting trapped in pools created during oil production, which they mistake for water. They struggle for several days to escape from the oily liquid, and when they die their bodies – and later their skeletons – remain suspended on the surface. In 1992 a law was passed forbidding the creation of new pools.

9437
The year started badly for the Shetland Islands, off the northeast coast of Scotland. After its engines had failed in heavy weather, the Liberian oil tanker Braer was hurled upon the rocky coast, where it broke into four pieces. About 85,000 tons of crude oil flowed into the North Sea, making it the worst environmental disaster in the region in 25 years.

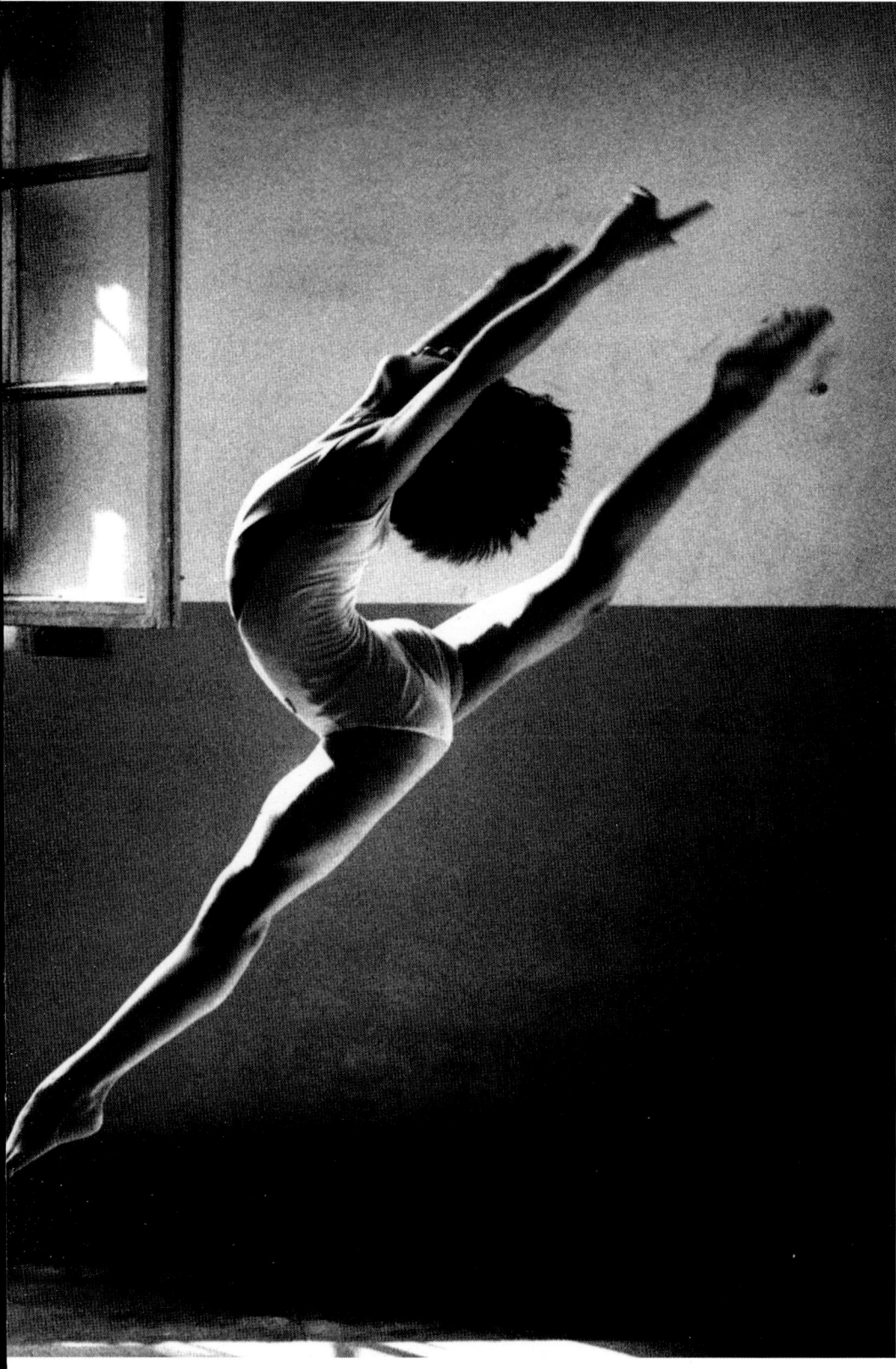

TOM STODDART
Katz Pictures,
UK

SECOND PRIZE
SINGLES (left)

SECOND PRIZE
STORIES

9440

9440
At special sports schools in China, girls bare-
ly out of kindergarten are subjected to a strict
regime designed to push the elasticity of the
human body to its limits. Their goal: Olympic
and/or world titles in gymnastics tourna-
ments. Above: A moment of grace and beauty
in a young life dominated by self-discipline
and pain (story continues).

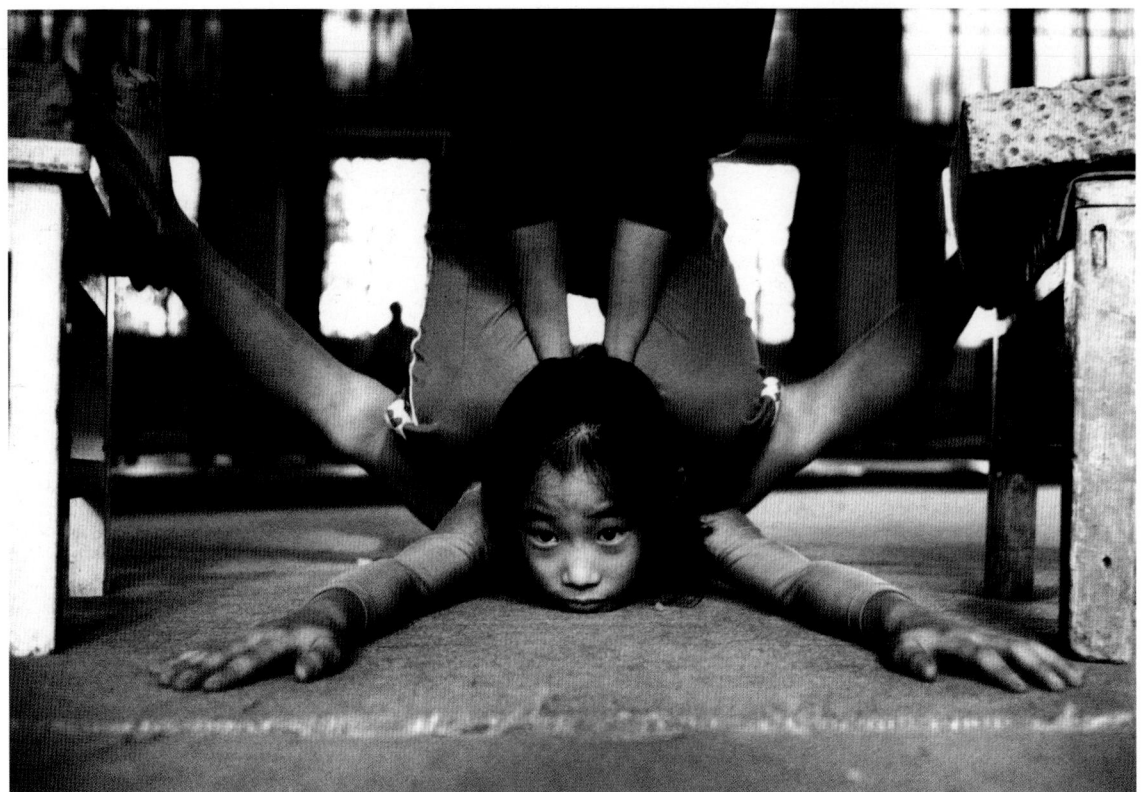

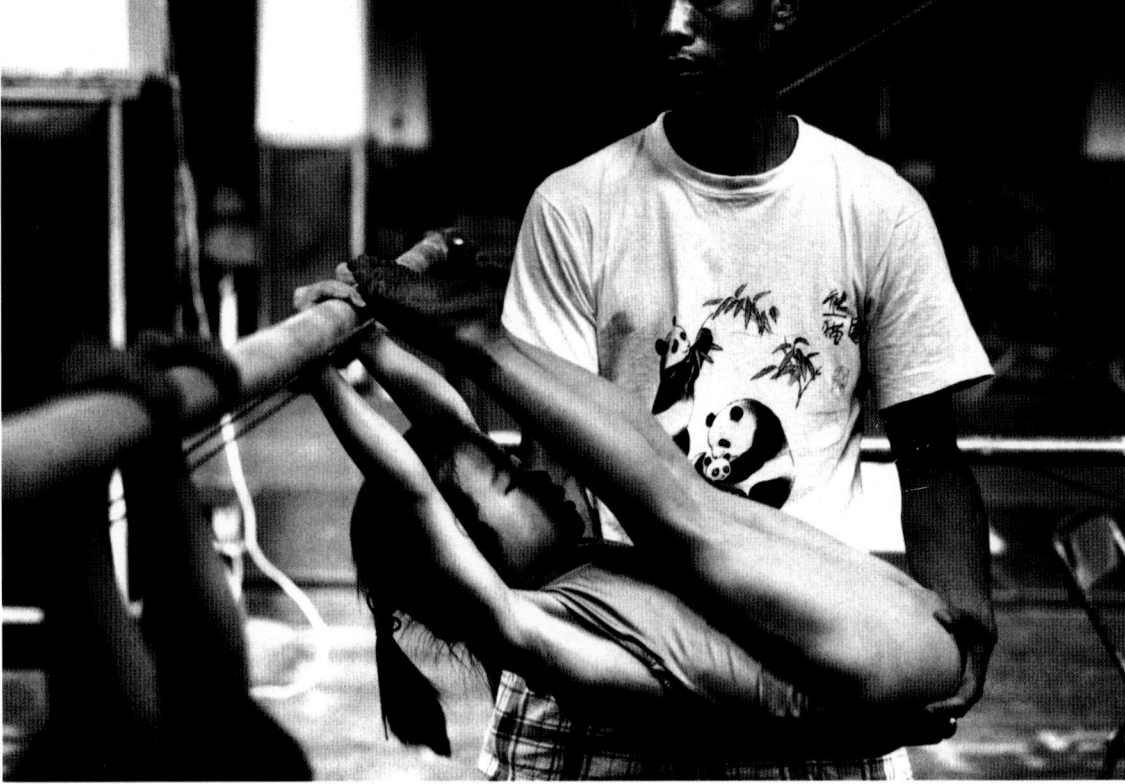

9440 (continued)
Programmed for success: at the sports school in Beijing the day begins at 5.30 a.m. A strict timetable tailored around at least four hours of training a day fits in schooling, rest and meals composed more for their nutritional value than their taste. The lights are switched off at 9 p.m.

The girls are groomed to reach their peak when they are 14 or 15 years old. Children from remote rural areas, who have developed willpower and discipline at an early age, score particularly highly at the school. The calluses on their hands tell their own story.

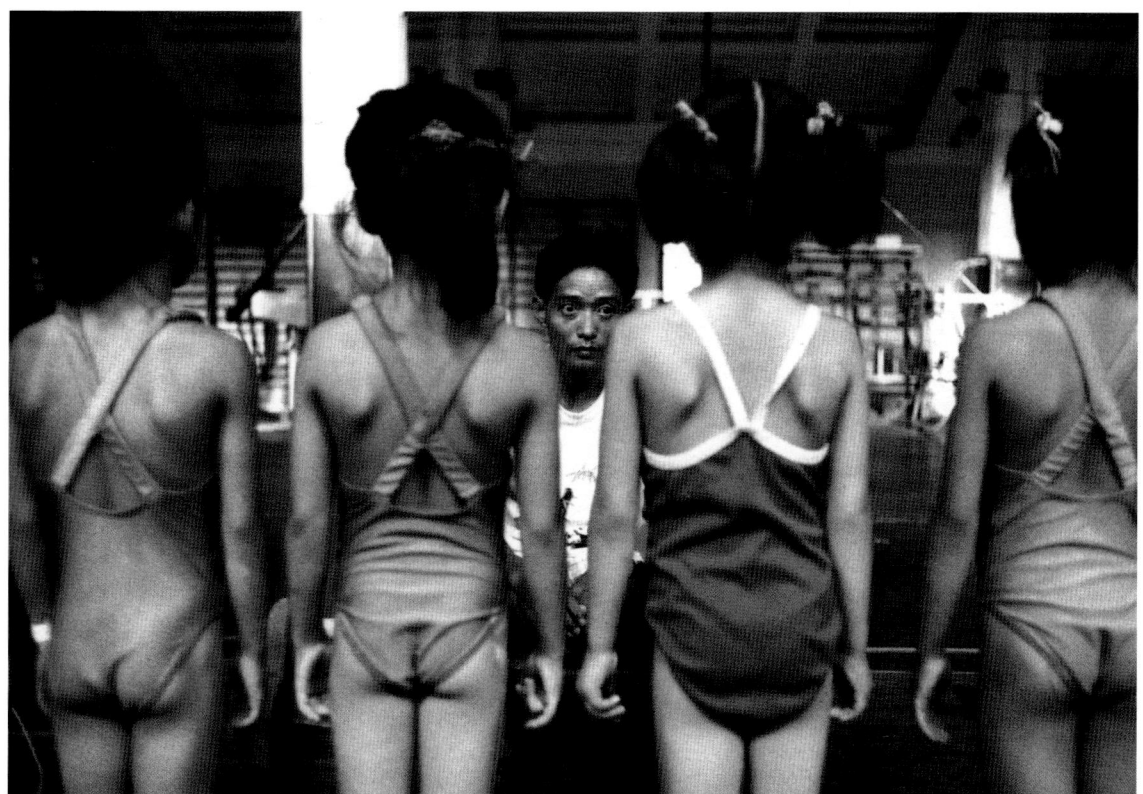

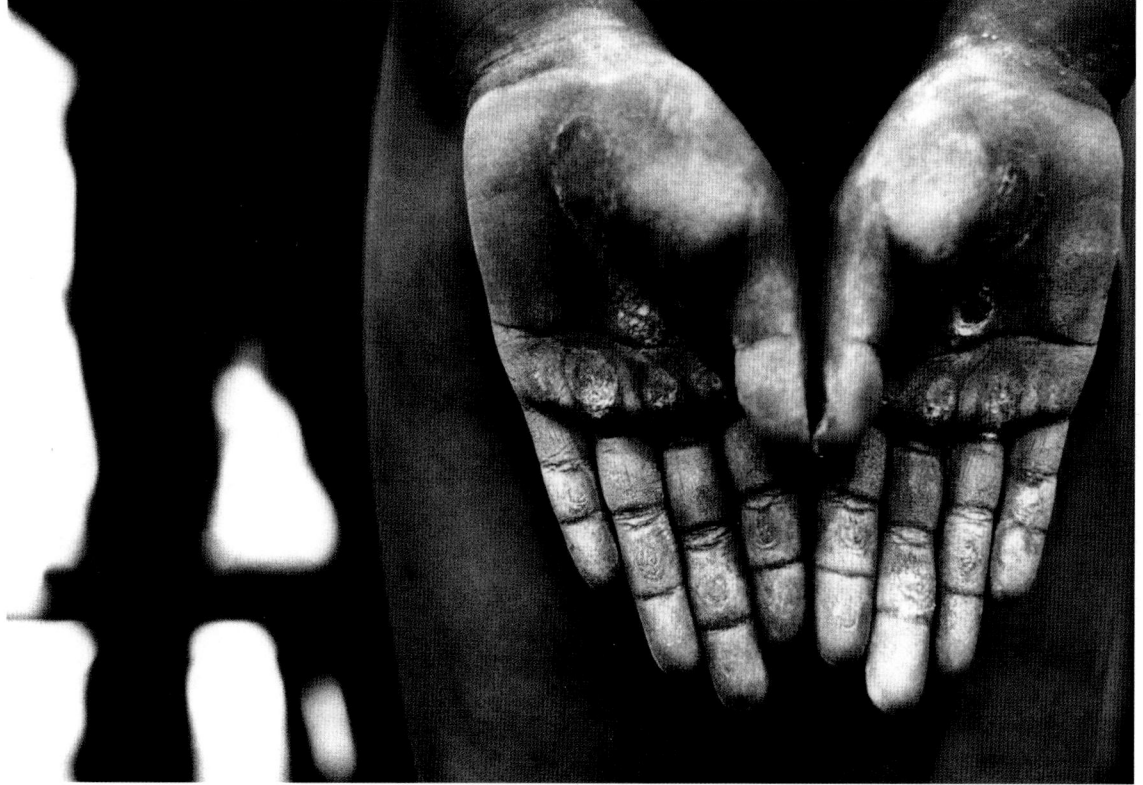

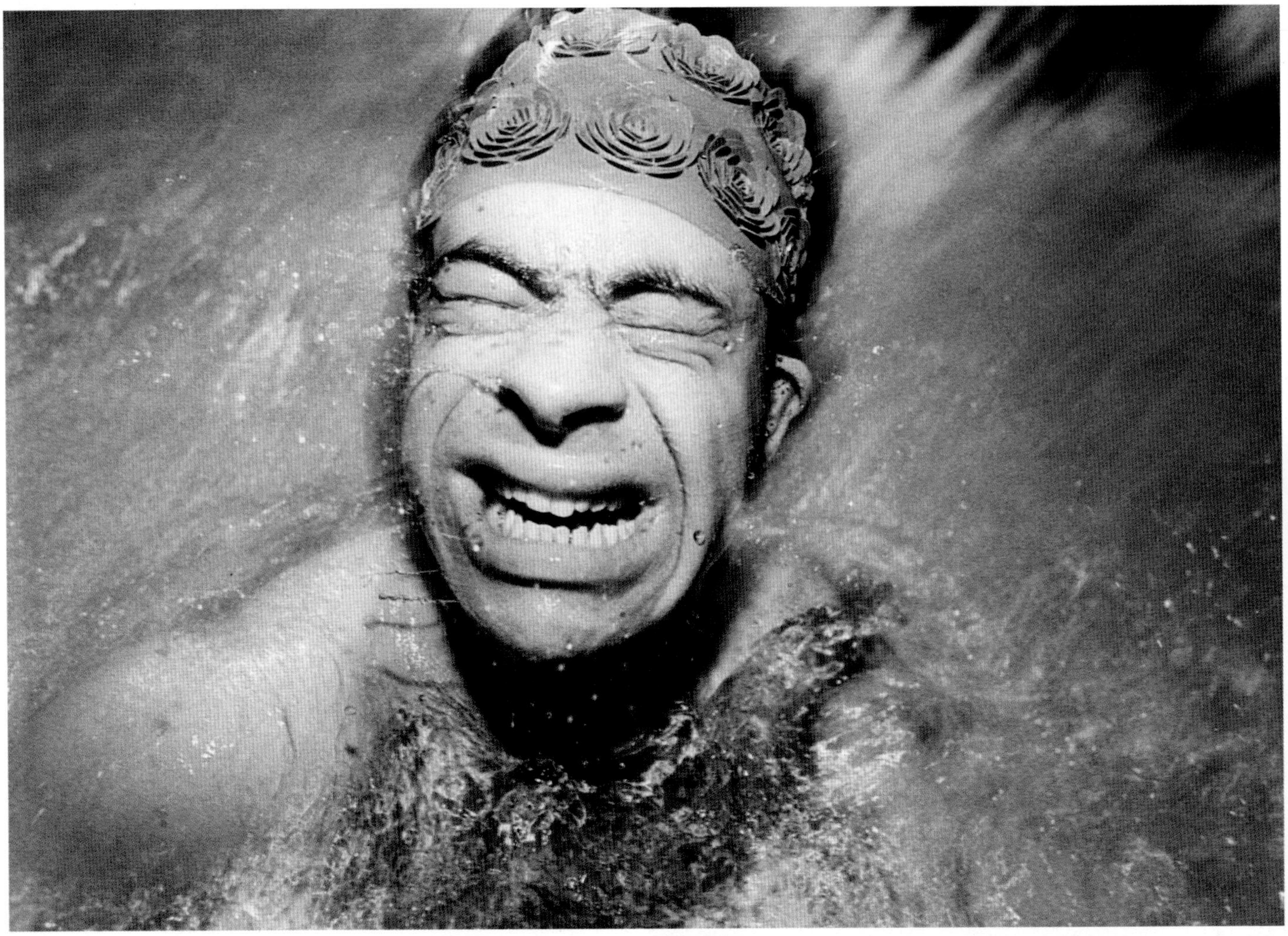

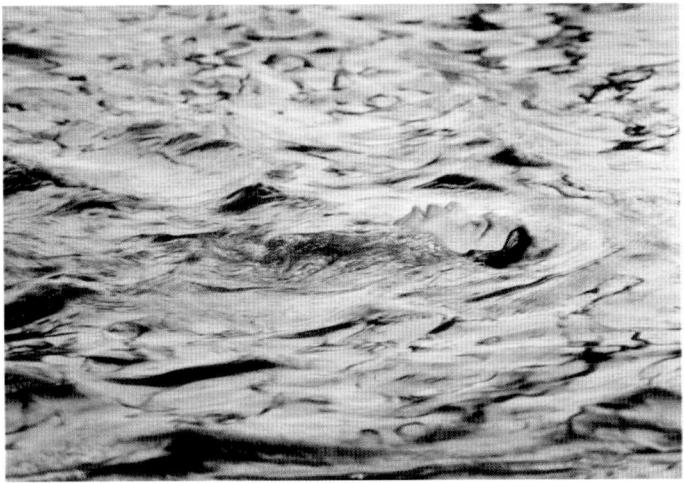
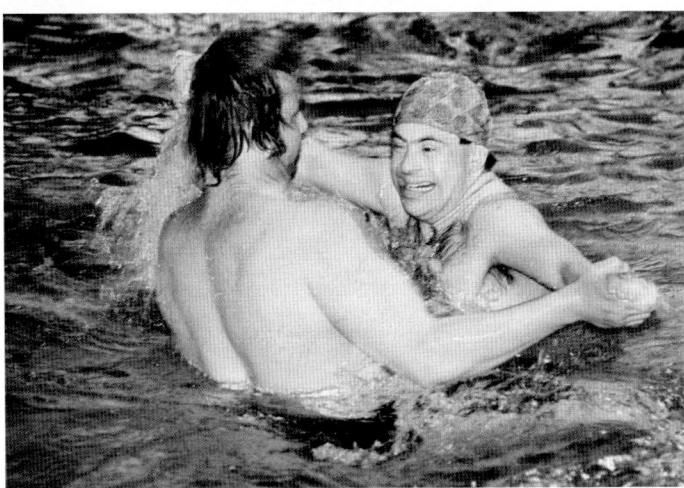

ROMAN SEJKOT
Your Artillery,
Czech Republic

**THIRD PRIZE
STORIES**

9441

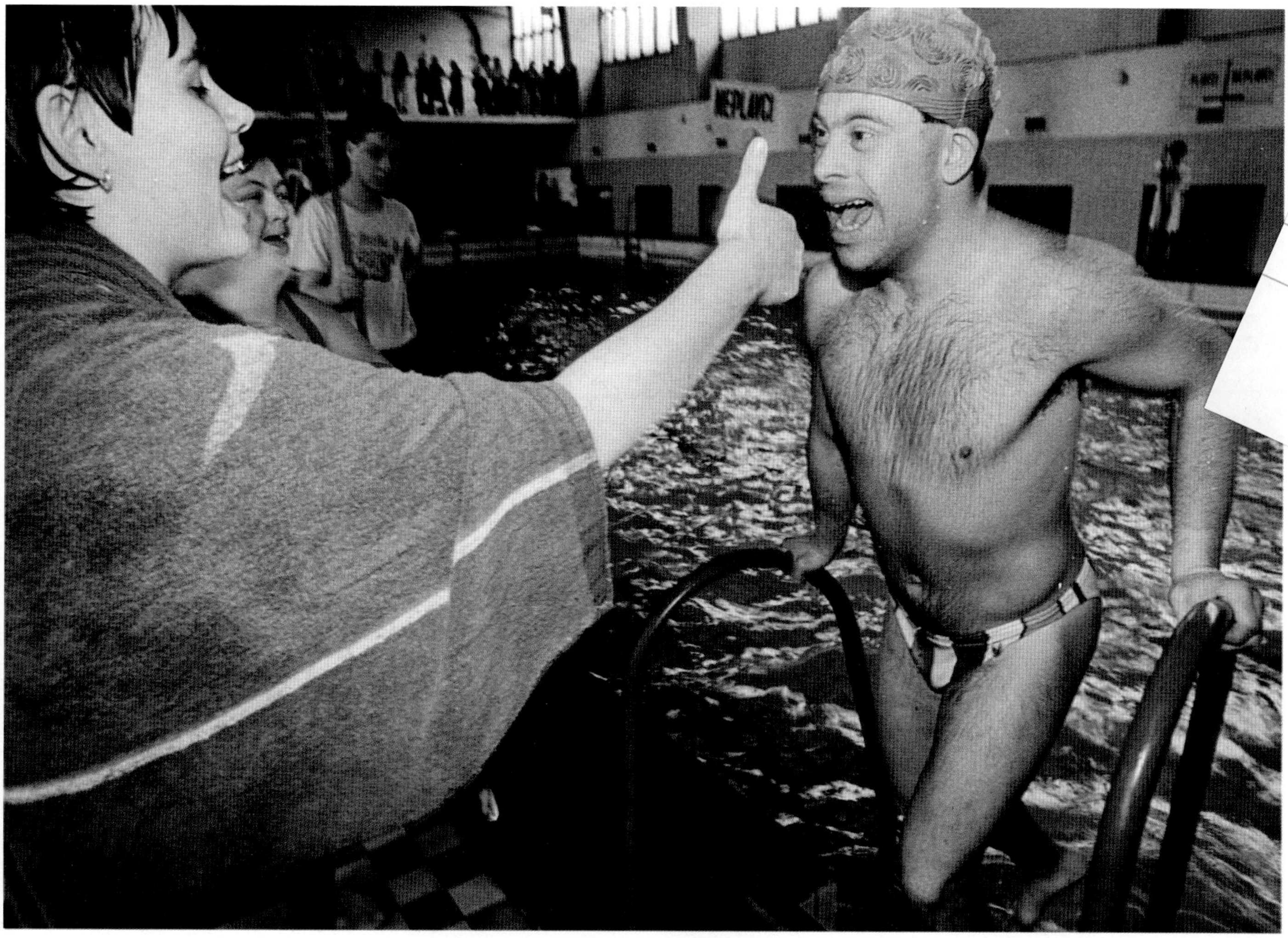

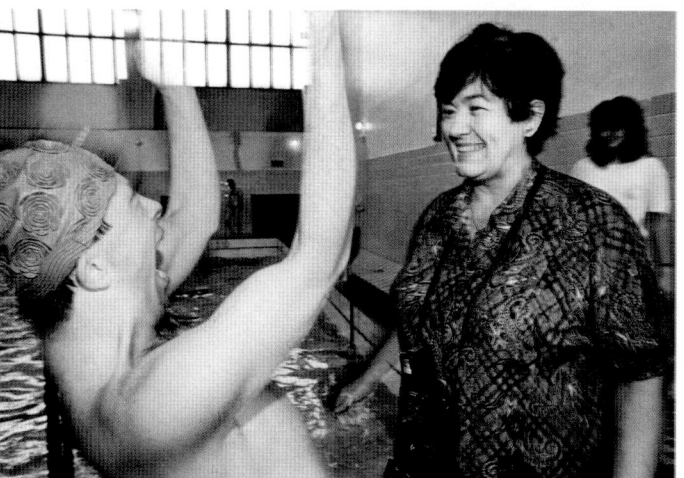

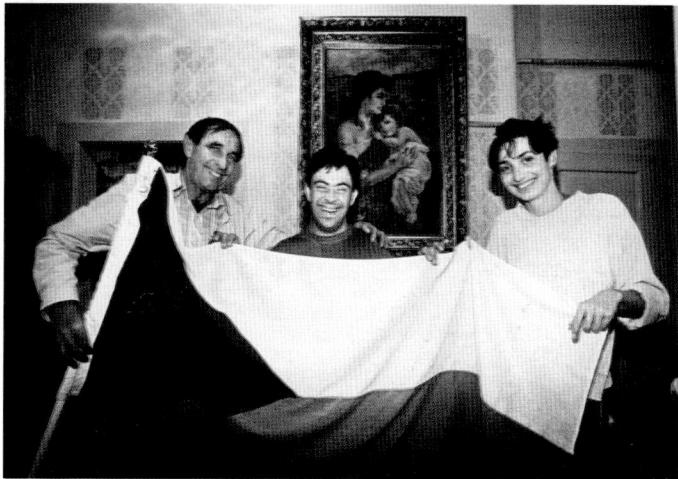

9441

This is the story of Bronislav Zemek, a mentally handicapped 23-year-old from Prague. Afflicted with Down's syndrome, he was afraid of water as a child. But he overcame his fear, started swimming when he was 12, and soon showed a keen taste for competition.

It was this fighting spirit that got Zemek selected to represent his country at the first Paralympiad for the mentally disabled in Madrid. Although he had never competed in a race before, he set the first Czech record on the 200 meters breast stroke.

TIM CLAYTON
Sydney
Morning Herald,
Australia

**FIRST PRIZE
SINGLES**

9442

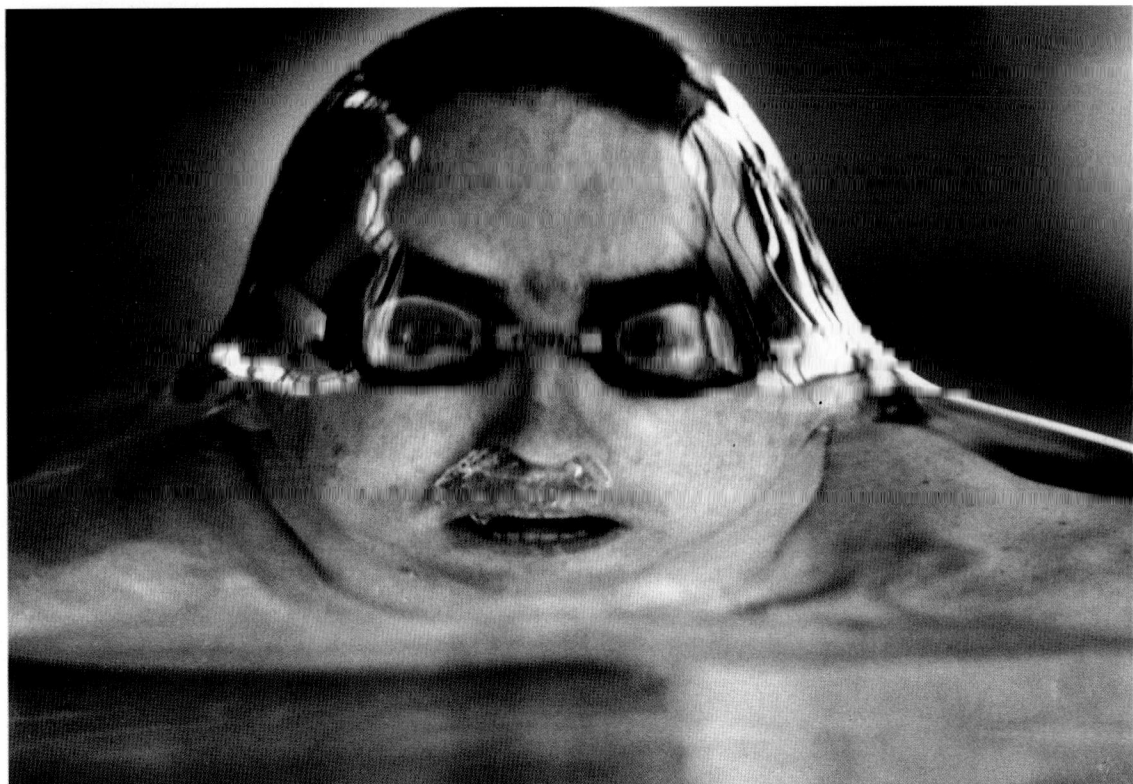

**MICHELE
MCDONALD**
Boston Globe,
USA

9443

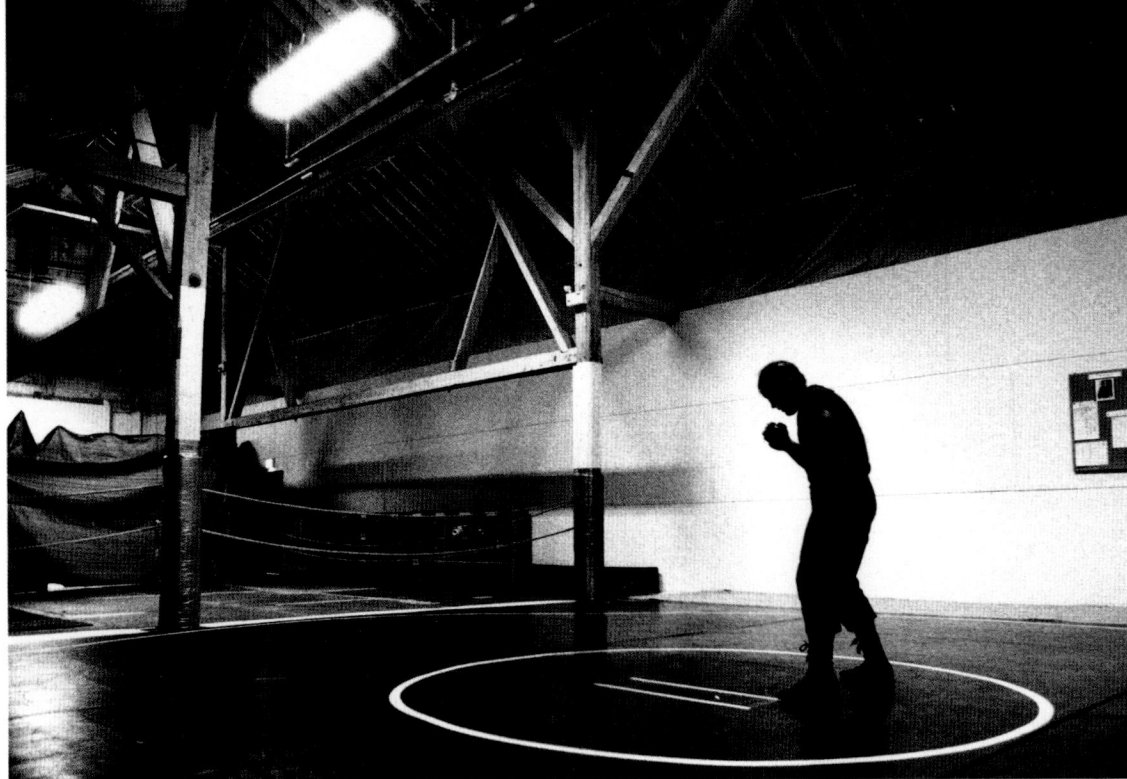

9442
Full stretch. Olympic 200-meter individual medley finalist Matthew Dunn was pictured during a training session in Sydney. The 'glassy' effect is caused by the surface tension of the water, which is about to be broken by the thrust of the swimmer's head.

9443
The loneliness of the professional boxer. Since losing his New England heavyweight title, Marc Machain's career appeared to have petered out. Then he decided to make one last attempt to break out of 'Pugsville', the world of nameless boxing pros. He gave all he'd got, but was beaten in the seventh round by a boxer seven years his junior.

ANNE CUSACK
Los Angeles Times,
USA

**THIRD PRIZE
SINGLES**

9444

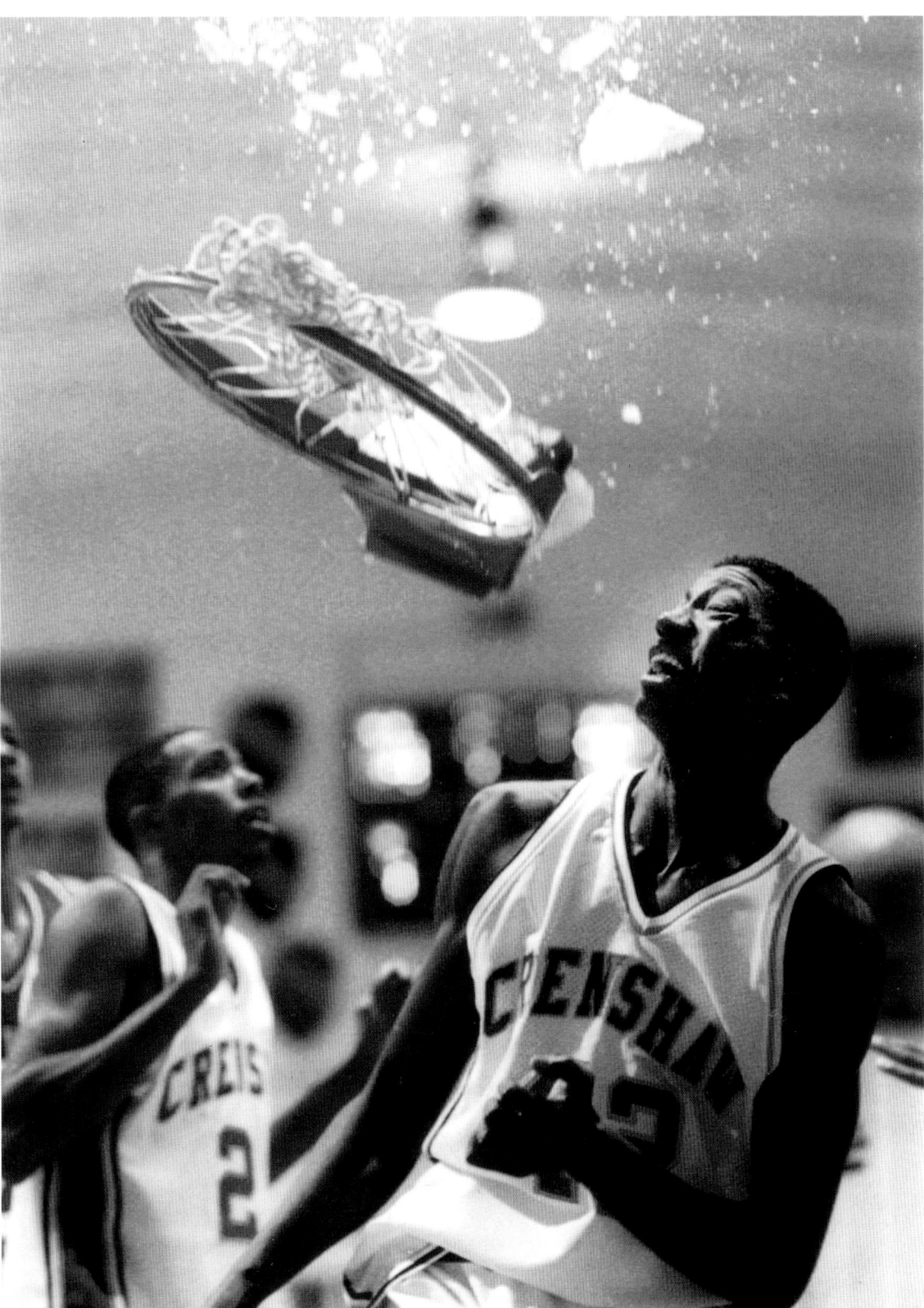

9444
During a basketball game at Thousand Oaks,
California, Leon Watson's 'slam dunk' was
executed with such force that the backboard
shattered and came crashing down on him -
he had to go to hospital for stitches. The
game between two high-school teams, the
Crenshaw Cougars and the Faith Baptists,
had to be abandoned.

GIDEON MENDEL
Germany/South
Africa,Network
Photographers for
Telegraph Magazine,
UK/Das Magazin,
Switzerland

**FIRST PRIZE
STORIES**

9445

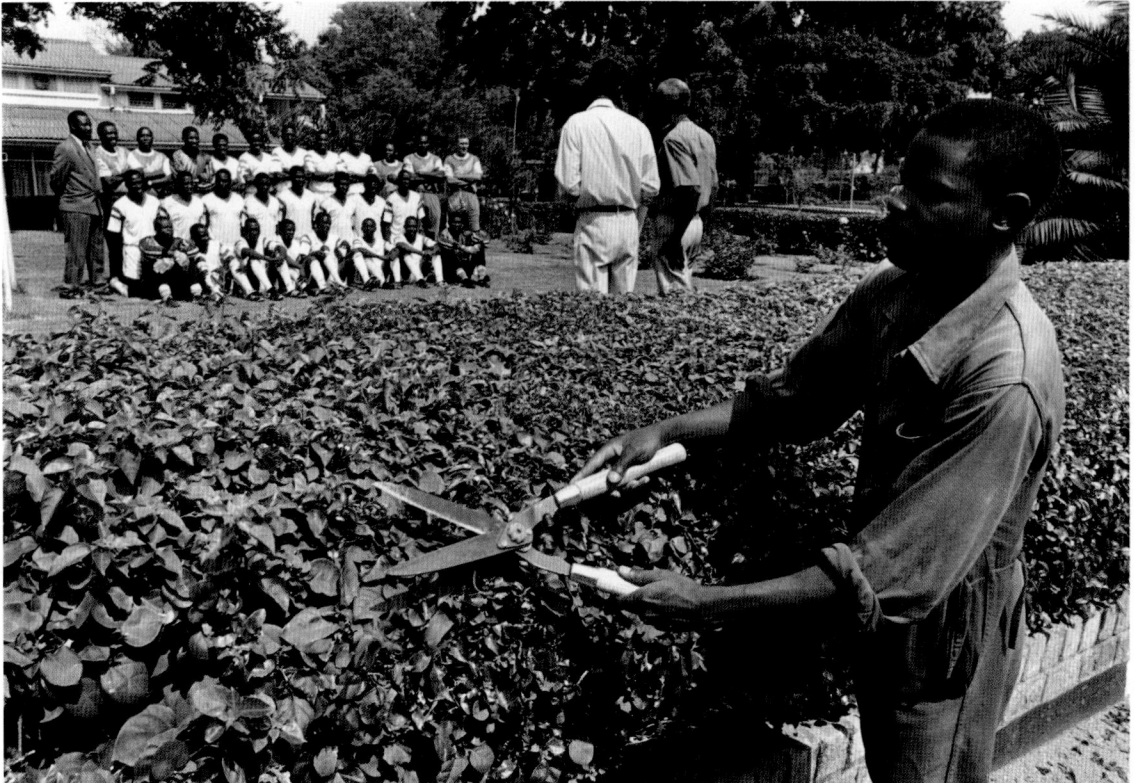

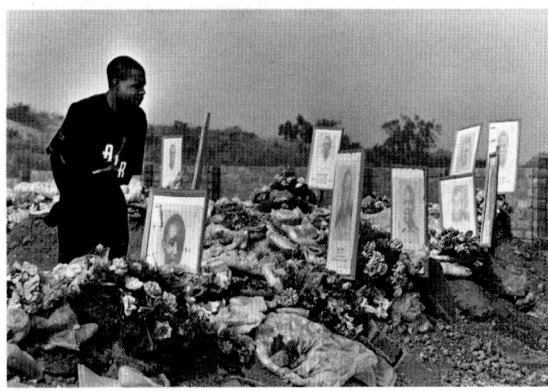

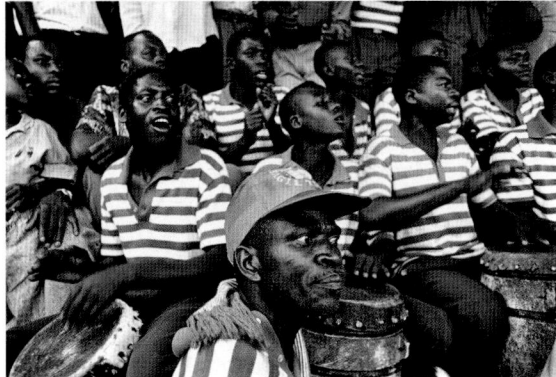

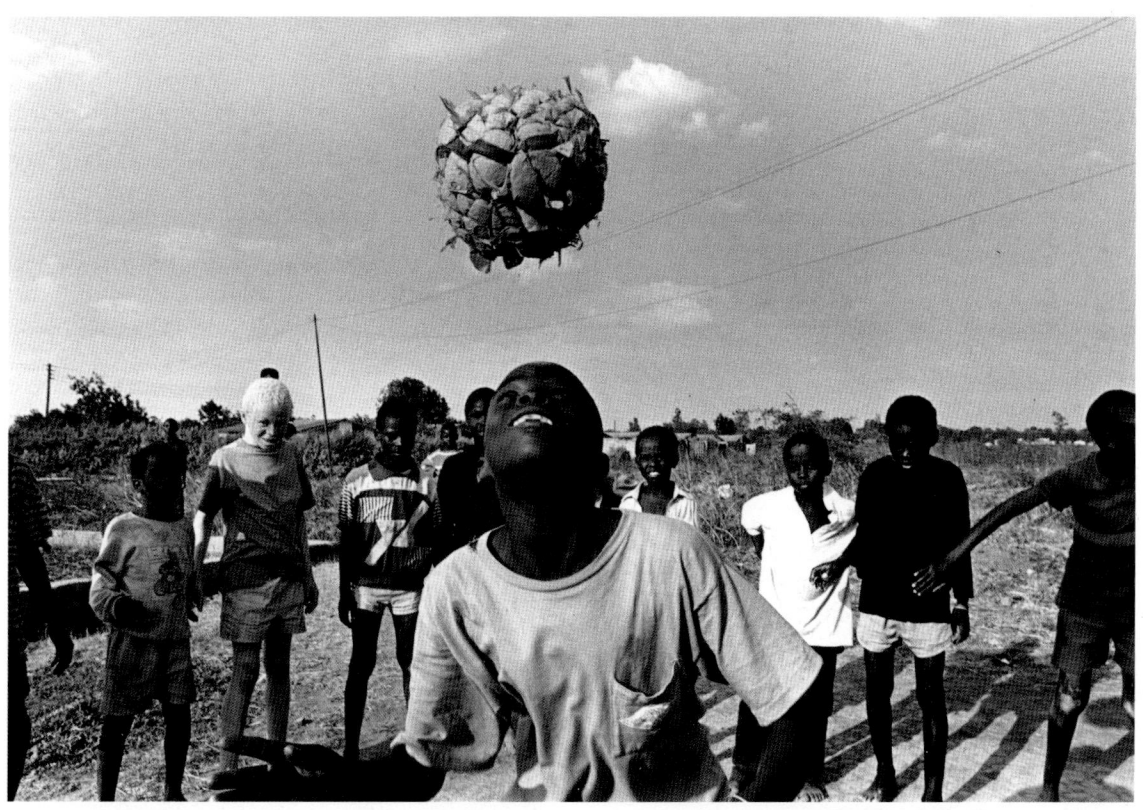

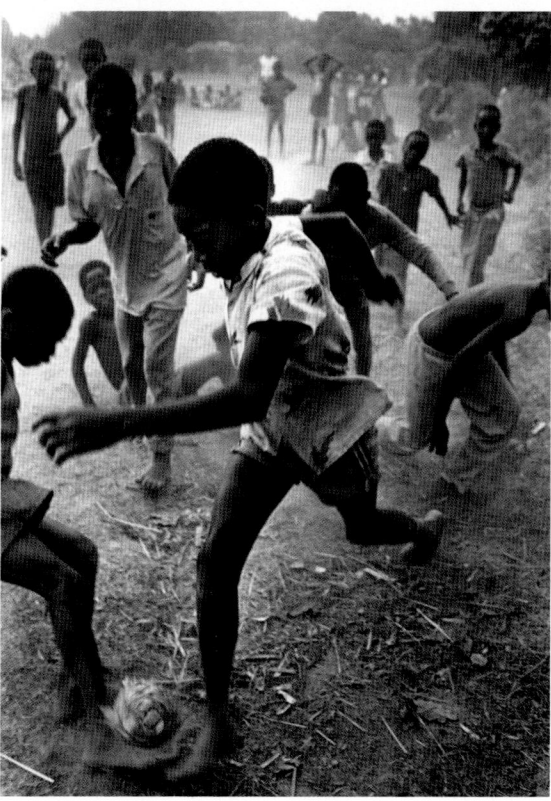

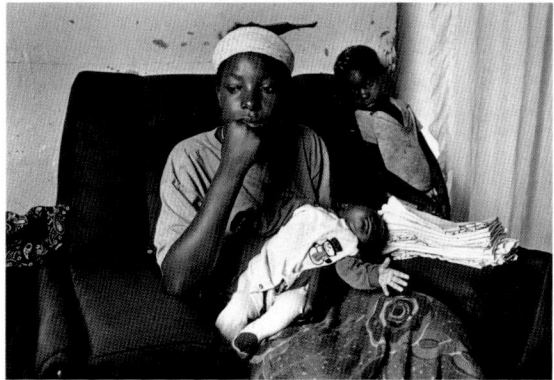

9445

Six months before this reportage was made, Zambia's national football team had perished in a plane crash in Gabon. The southern African country showed its resilience by putting together a new national selection in record time. The team narrowly failed to qualify for the World Cup tournament in the USA.

Far left: The captain of both the old team and the new (which poses for photographers at top left) lingers at the burial place of his former teammates. This page: Young players practice their skills with a homemade ball, and the widow and baby of one of those killed. Next pages: The new goalkeeper after the match that cost Zambia its place in the World Cup.

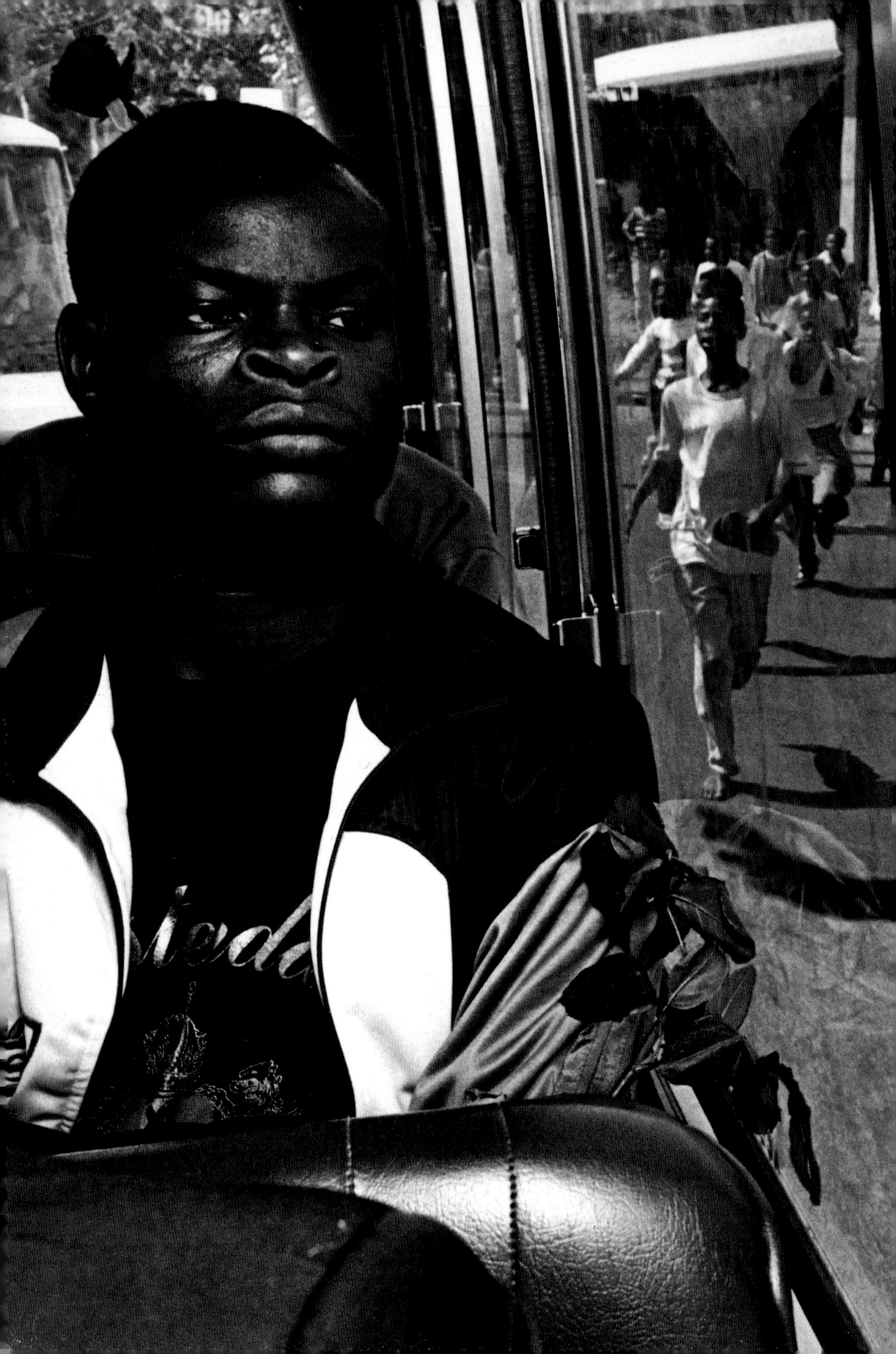

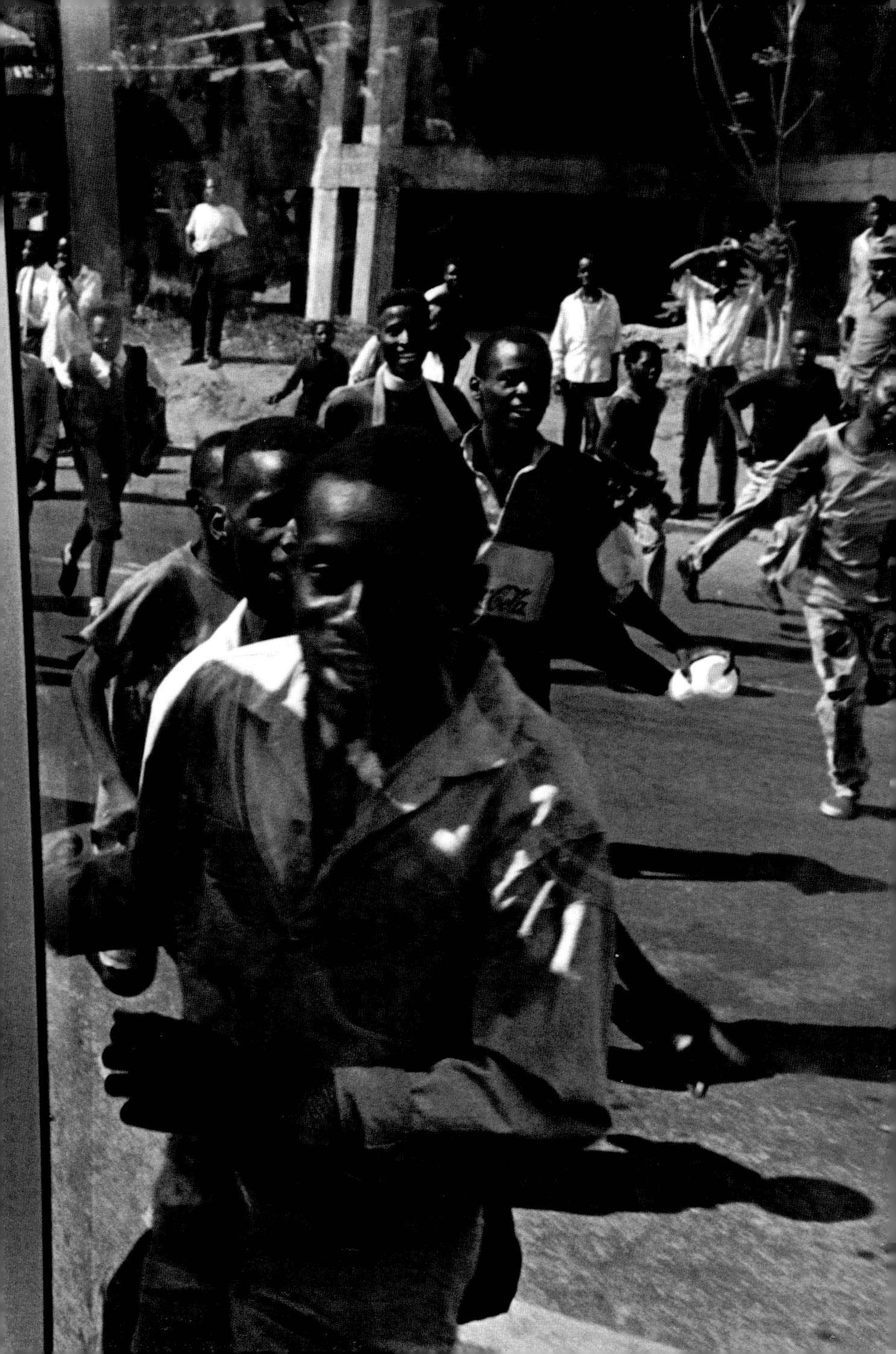

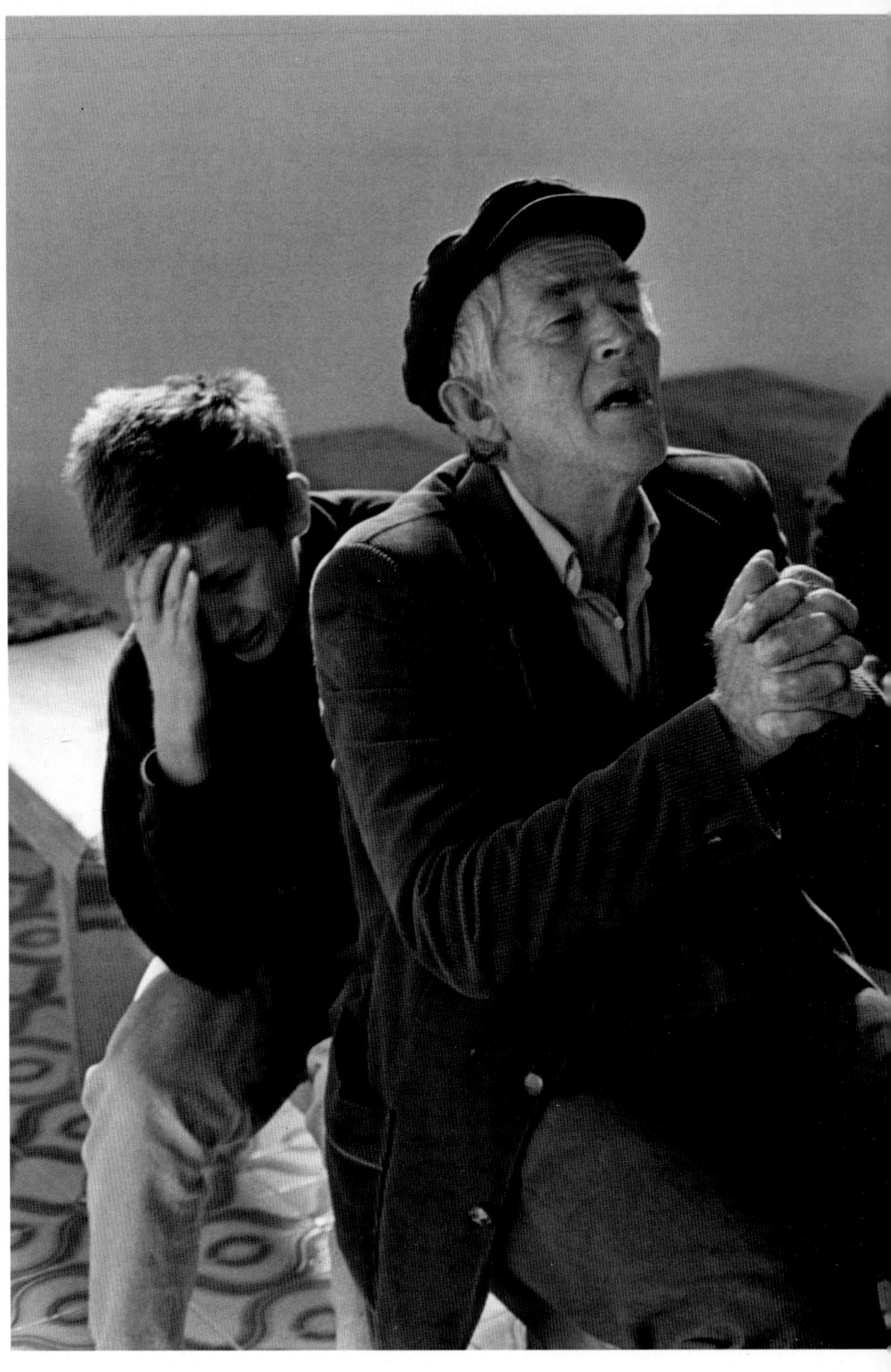

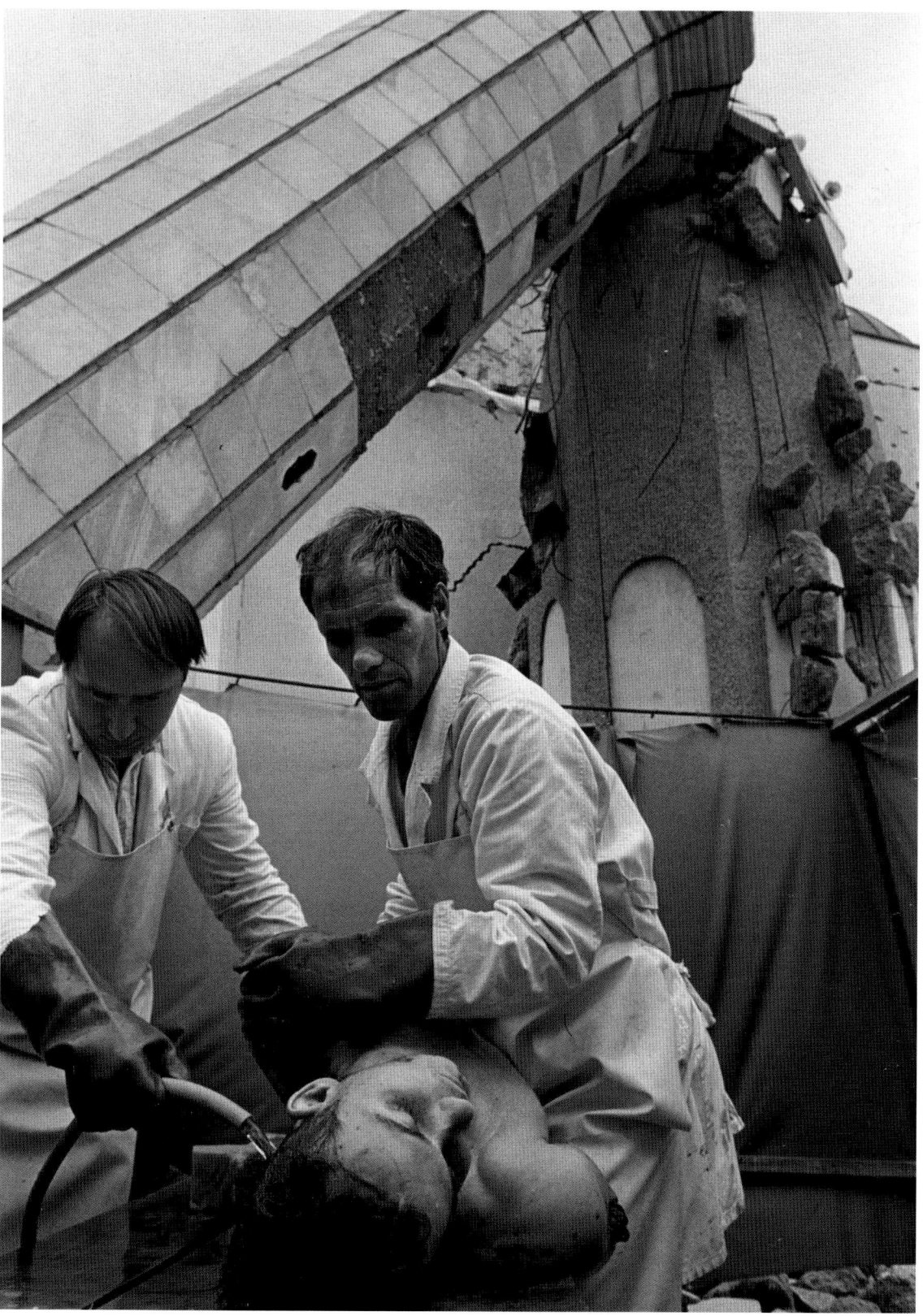

9449
In May, the photographer spent several weeks in the battlefields of northern Bosnia near the town of Brčko. In an attempt to widen their land link with Serbia, Serb forces pushed past the defenders of the Muslim villages they found in their way. The sustained hostilities turned peasants into veteran fighters.

They had to pay a terrible price. At makeshift mortuaries and ever-expanding cemeteries, where the victims of the daily horror are washed and buried, relatives and friends mourn their dead (bottom left and next page). Above, medics attend to a casualty at the foot of a minaret broken in two by Serbian shelling (story continues).

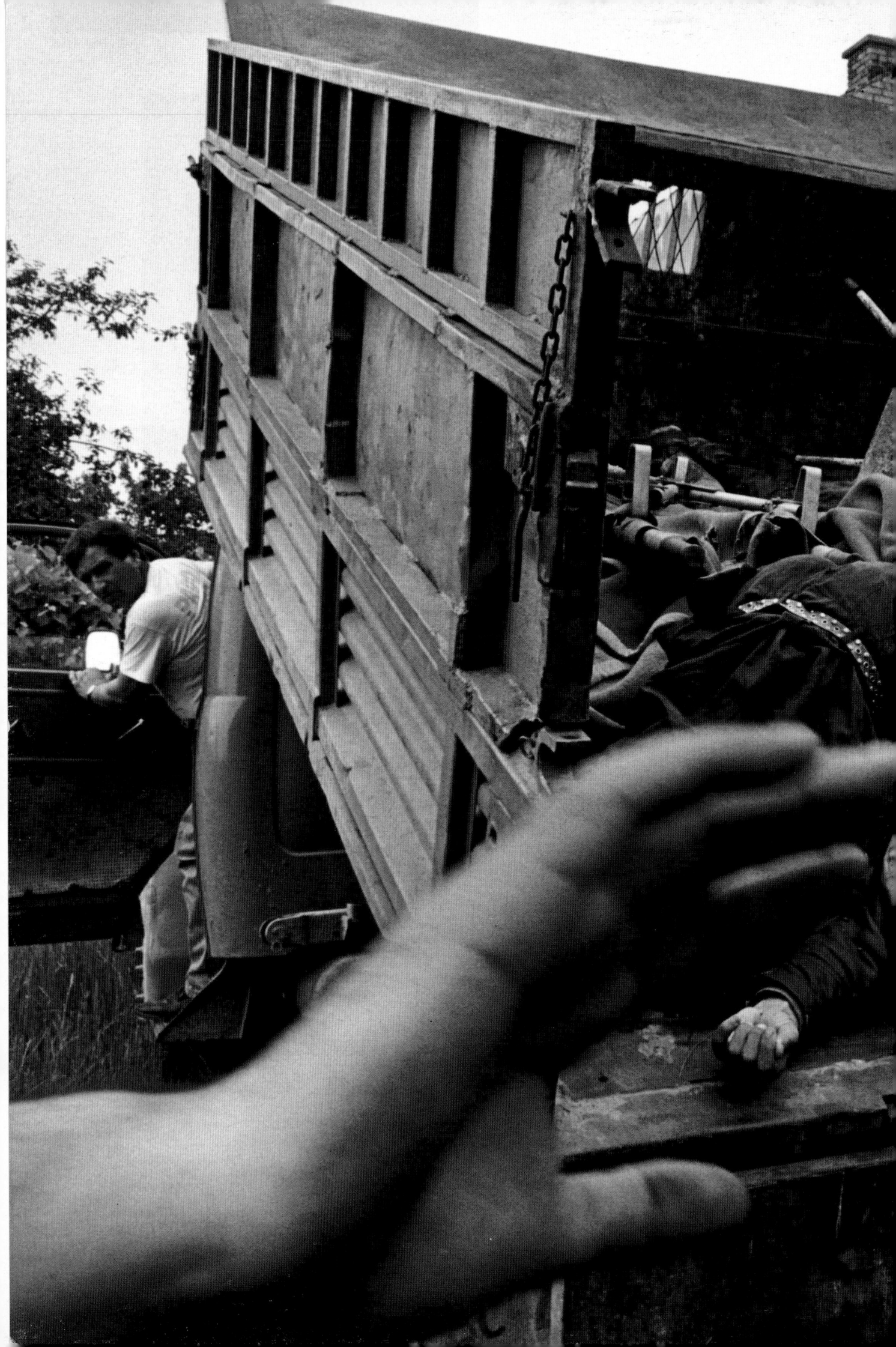

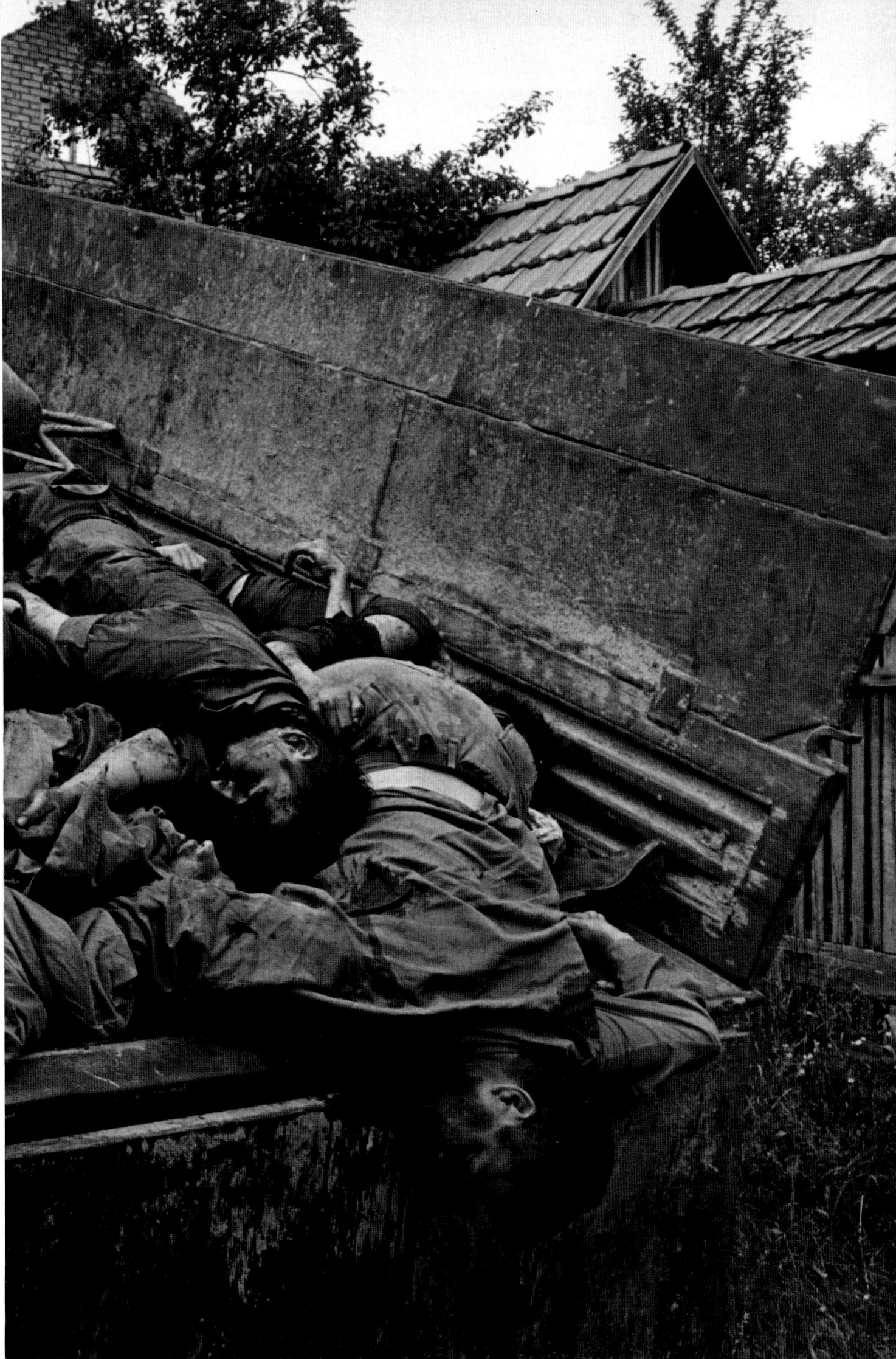

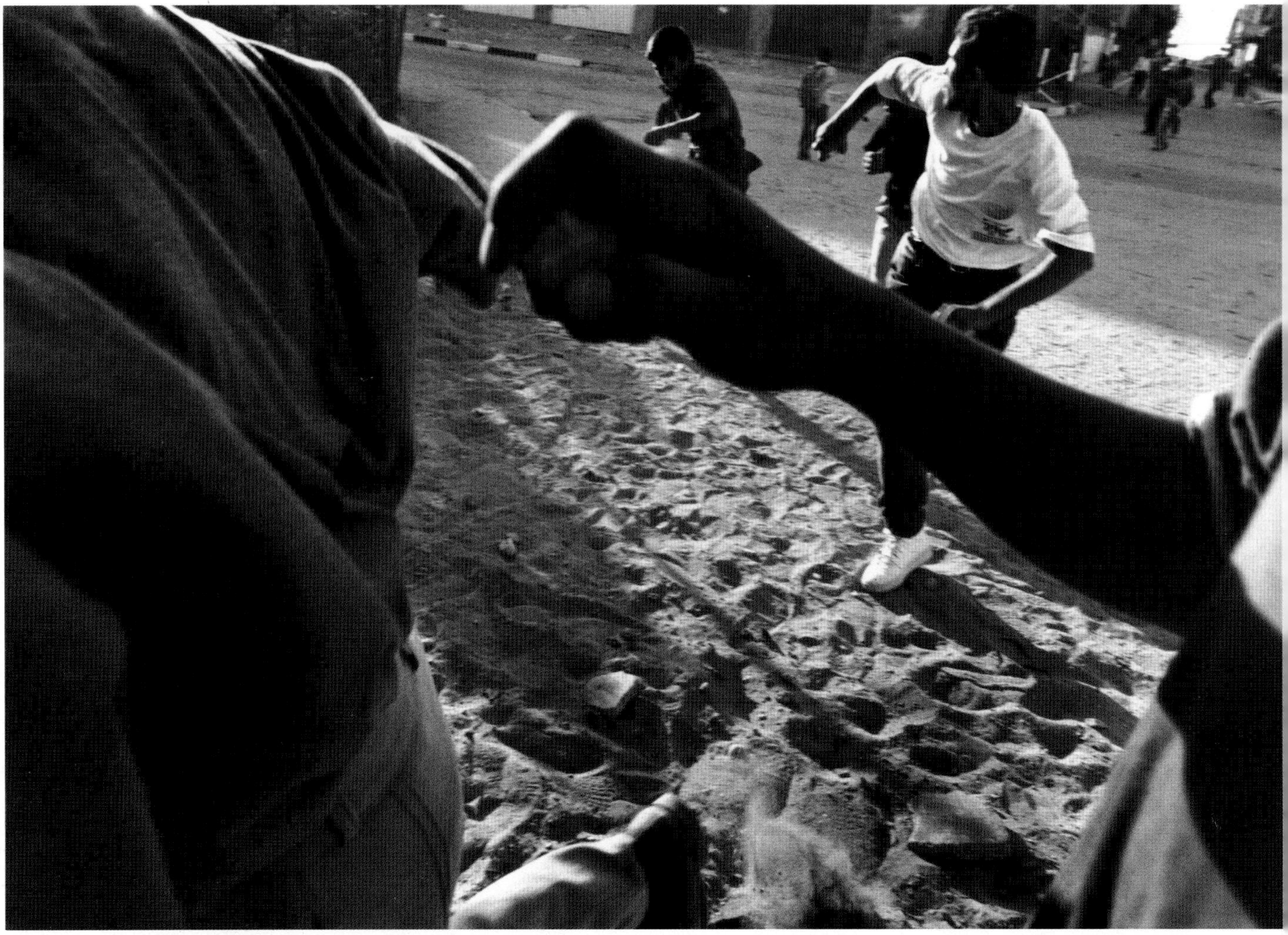

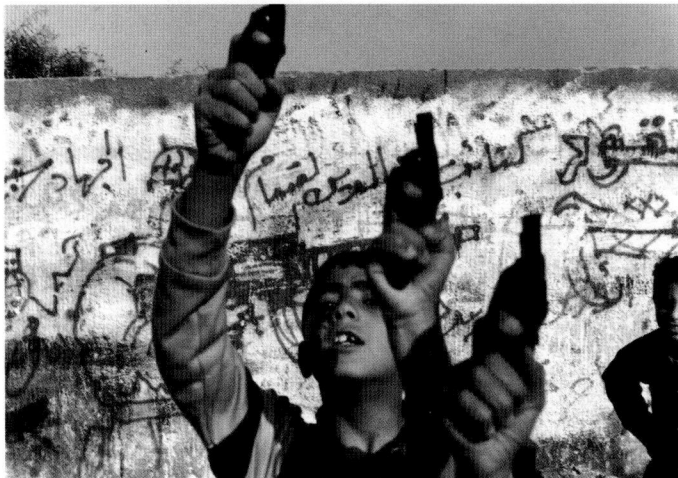

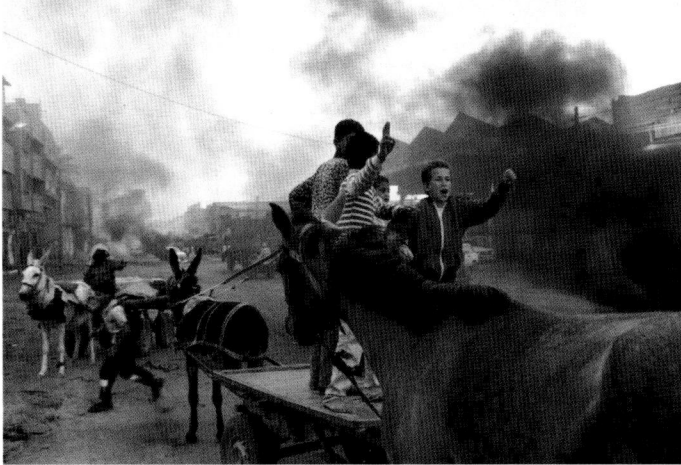

LARRY TOWELL
Canada,
Magnum Photos,
USA

**FIRST PRIZE
STORIES**

9453

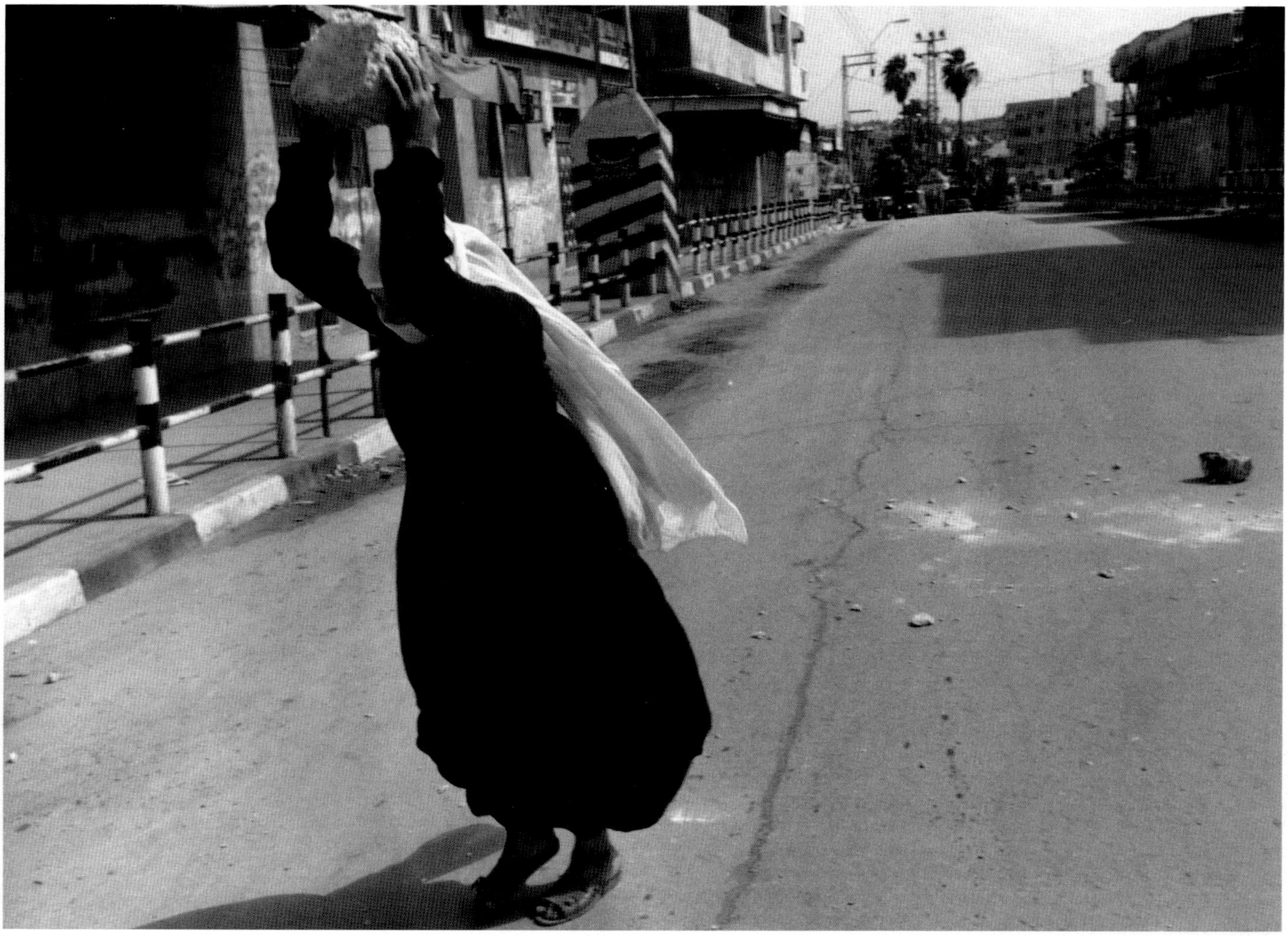

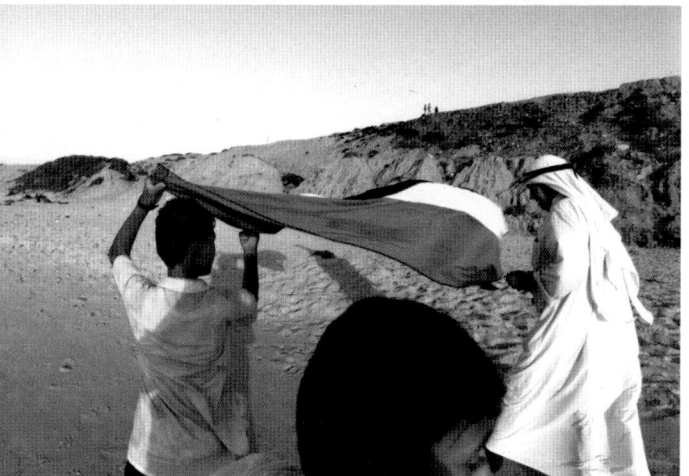

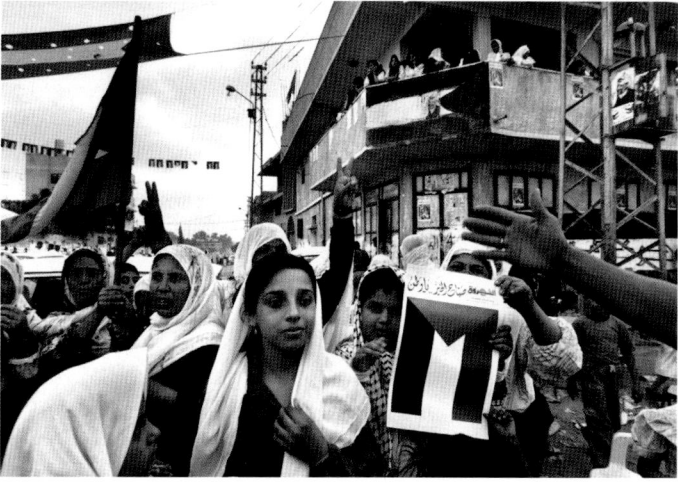

9453
Begun long before Rabin and Arafat signed their peace accord in Washington, this reportage covers life in the occupied Gaza Strip and East Jerusalem. Palestinians of all ages play their part in the Intifada (top and bottom left). Israeli repercussions often have people scrambling for cover (facing page, top).

The violence reached a peak in May, when 30 Palestinians were killed and hundreds injured. But the announcement of the peace agreement brought hope to the strife-torn area. As nationalist sentiment ran high, both sides unfurled their flags. Following pages: In East Jerusalem, Israelis proclaim their God-given right to a 'greater Israel'.

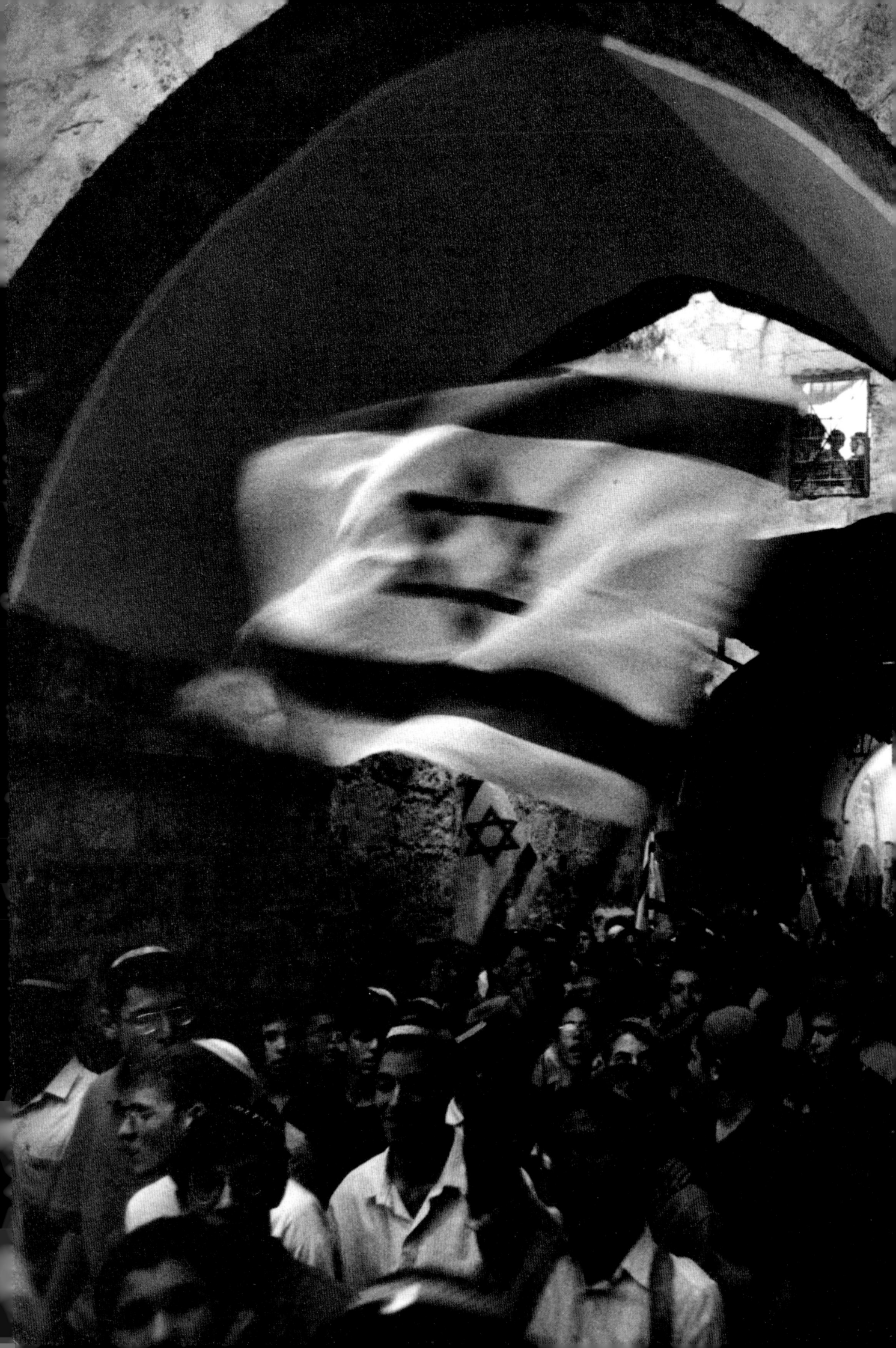

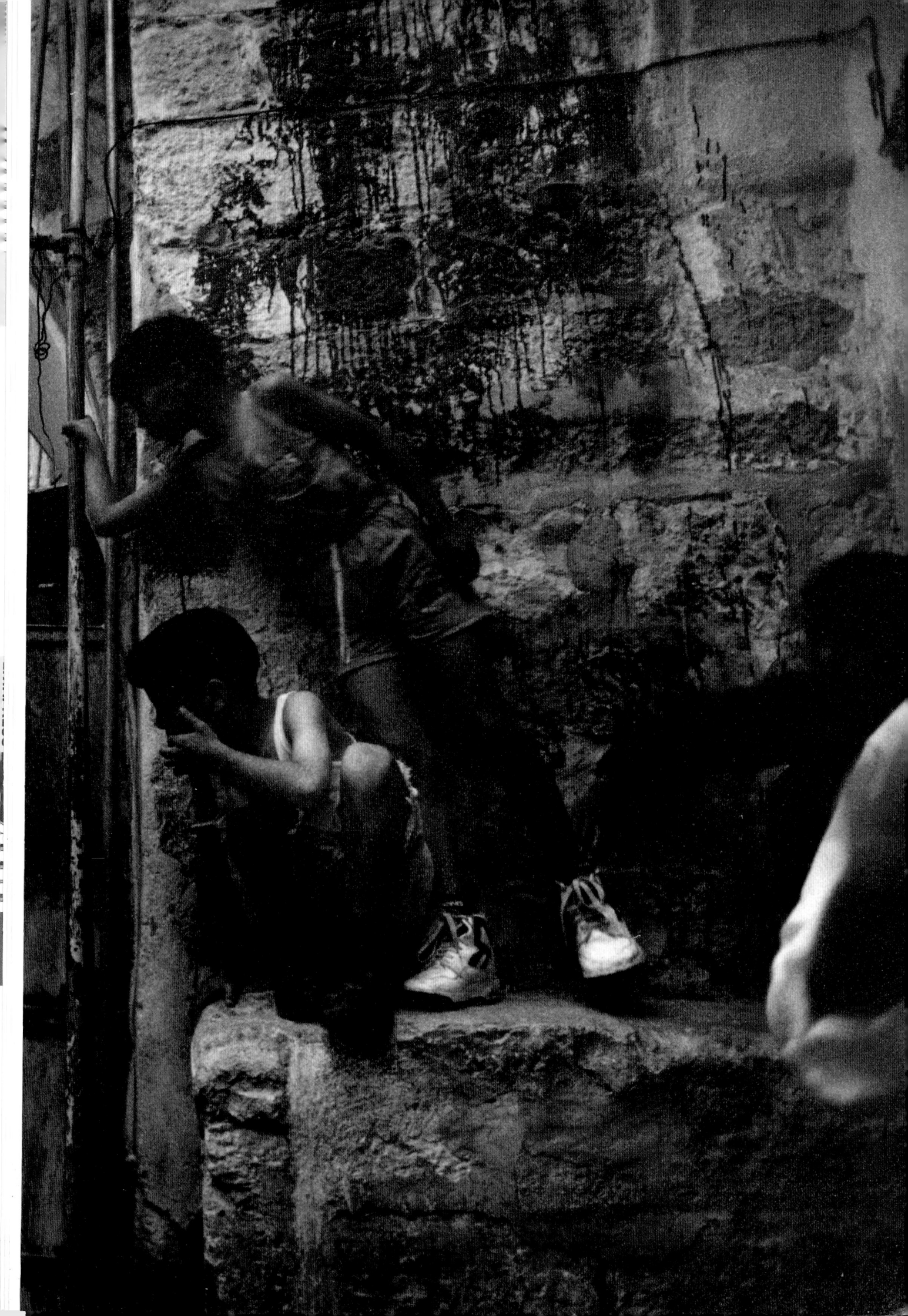

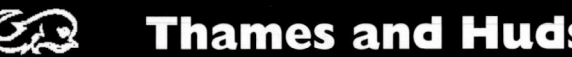
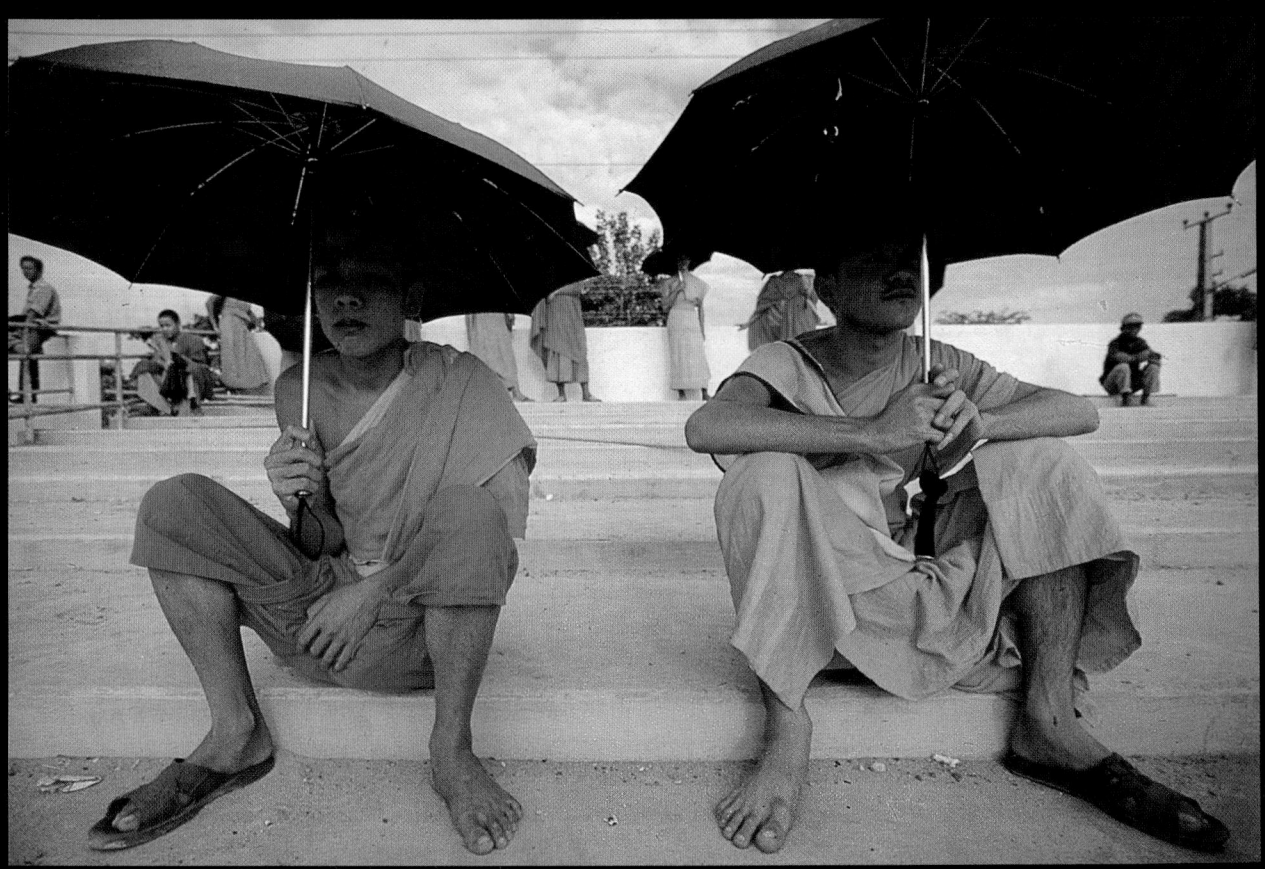

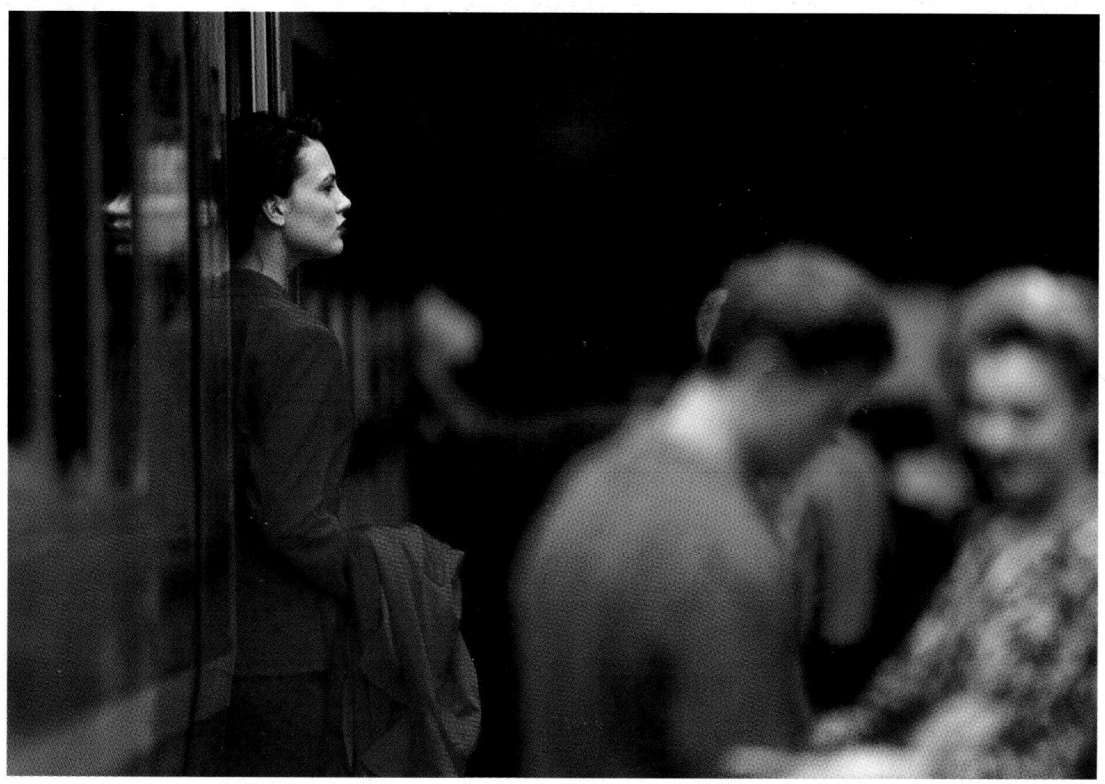

The advantages of eye-controlled AF are immediately apparent.

Think fast. It's a requirement of all fast-action photography, and you'd best be prepared to act. The EOS 5 is. It introduces Canon's unique Eye-Controlled Autofocus. Any one of five focusing points can be selected simply by looking at the corresponding AF frame in the viewfinder. One look and you're ready to shoot. It's that easy. And that fast.

The brain of the camera is a 16-bit microprocessor. You get more from the brain when you pair it with one of Canon's equally fast **ULTRASONIC** motor lenses. While designed for the profes-

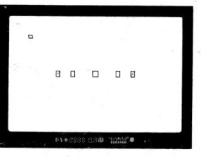

sional or high-amateur, the EOS 5 is easy to handle. Three dials control most of the functions. Leaving you free to shoot whatever catches your eye.

- 1/8000 sec shutter speed
- 16-zone metering sensor
- Built-in auto zoom flash
- 16 custom functions
- Predictive AF
- Whisper-quiet film transport

THE CREATIVE EYE

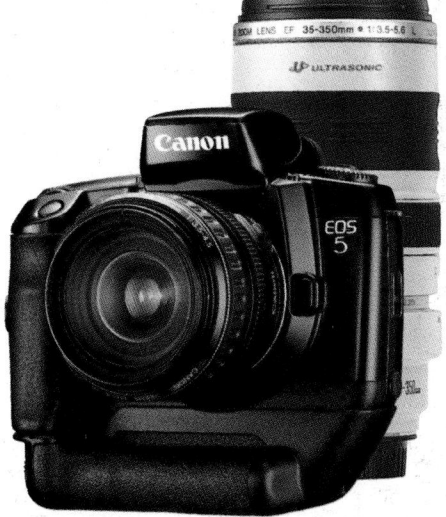

Vertical Holding Grip (optional)

Canon EOS 5

Canon Europa N.V., P.O. Box 2262, 1180 EG Amstelveen, the Netherlands

© World Press Photo Holland
Foundation
Sdu Publishers Koninginnegracht,
The Hague

First published in Great Britain
in 1994 by Thames and Hudson Ltd.,
London

First published in the United States
of America in 1994 by
Thames and Hudson Inc.,
500 Fifth Avenue, New York,
New York 10110

Art director
Hans van Blommestein
Designer
Louis Voogt
Picture coordinators
Ben ten Berge
Ilan Roos
Linda Steuernagel
Caption writer
Terri James-Kester
Supervising editor
Kari Lundelin

Lithography
Nefli b.v., Haarlem
Paper
KNP Fine Paper Division, Maastricht
Proost en Brandt, Diemen
Printing
Sdu Grafische Projecten, The Hague
Binding
Hexspoor, Boxtel
Production supervisor
Rob van Zweden,
Sdu Publishers Koninginnegracht,
The Hague

This book has been published under
the auspices of the World Press Photo
Holland Foundation.

**British Library Cataloguing-in-
Publication Data**
A catalogue-record for this book is
available from The British Library
ISBN 0-500-97412-8

**World Press Photo
Van Baerlestraat 144
1071 BE Amsterdam**
The Netherlands
Telephone +31 (20) 6766 096
Fax   +31 (20) 6764 471
Telex 10611 aoc nl att. WPPh
Managing director: Marloes Krijnen

Cover
Antoine Gyori,
France, Sygma
'Orphan in Sarajevo,
January 1993'

Title page
Jim Mendenhall,
USA, Los Angeles Times
'Palm Tree Ablaze during Firestorm,
Southern California,
November 1993'

Back page
Thomas Dallal,
USA, JB Pictures
'Children Cheer Arafat and the Signing
of Palestinian/Israeli Peace Accord,
Gaza City, 13 September 1993'